Examberry

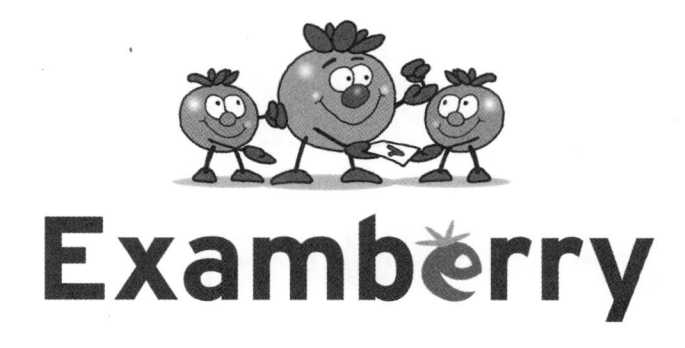

Advanced Level Vocabulary - Book 2

Introduction

So, why learn vocabulary? The simplest answer is that as human beings, our most common means of communication is language. It is through the use of language that we express our ideas, needs and emotions. Words are the building blocks we use to share our intelligence. Having a greater number of words allows us to communicate with each other in ever more elaborate, sophisticated and persuasive ways.

On a more mundane level, expanding vocabulary is vital for children sitting 11+ Grammar and Independent School entrance exams. In both types of exam there is an element of creative or descriptive writing in which examiners are specifically looking for evidence of a well-developed vocabulary.

An extensive vocabulary suggests a child is well and widely read and able to put forward ideas and arguments in an intelligent way that will be helpful in all areas of academic life, not just in English language lessons.

The most natural way to increase a child's vocabulary is through reading a wide variety of books. That way a child can pick up new words while seeing them used in context. However, this involves years of enthusiastic reading and not all children are natural bookworms.

If your child is not a great lover of reading, this book will help expose them to new words and the exercises included with each vocabulary list will encourage your child to use these words, in context, in real sentences.

As they work through the list you can support your child's learning by encouraging them to use the newly acquired words in everyday speech, perhaps when describing their day, an incident at school, or a favourite film. As your child begins to use these previously unfamiliar words they will become more confident about using them in their work and their expressive writing skills will quickly develop.

Good Luck!

© Examberry 2021

Examberry

Chapter 1	page 3
Chapter 2	page 6
Chapter 3	page 9
Chapter 4	page 12
Chapter 5	page 15
Chapter 6	page 18
Chapter 7	page 21
Chapter 8	page 24
Chapter 9	page 27
Chapter 10	page 30
Chapter 11	page 33
Chapter 12	page 36
Chapter 13	page 39
Chapter 14	page 42
Chapter 15	page 45
Chapter 16	page 48
Chapter 17	page 51
Chapter 18	page 54
Chapter 19	page 57
Chapter 20	page 60
Answers	page 63

© Examberry 2021

Vocabulary 1

Learn the following words and then answer the questions.

1. **Feline** (adj.): catlike, elegant, graceful, stealthy.
   The model walks with <u>feline</u> grace, even in high heels.

2. **Disgruntled** (adj.): a state of sulky dissatisfaction, resentful, sullen, annoyed.
   <u>Disgruntled</u> employees called for the director's resignation when he cut their salaries.

3. **Spurious** (adj.): counterfeit, bogus, fake.
   The stranger made a <u>spurious</u> claim about being a member of the Royal Family, which was later discovered to be false.

4. **Portray** (v.): represent, depict, imitate, express, illustrate.
   The lawyer <u>portrayed</u> his client as the victim of a vicious attack in order to evoke sympathy from the jury.

5. **Secluded** (adj.): isolated, sheltered, remote, lonely.
   There is a <u>secluded</u> spot in the hills where people often go to watch the sunset in peace.

6. **Nuptial** (adj.): relating to marriage, matrimonial, spousal.
   Wedding guests are asked to witness the couple's <u>nuptial</u> vows.

7. **Infuriate** (v.): make angry, enrage, inflame, madden.
   The students' constant chatter during his speech started to <u>infuriate</u> the Headmaster, so he gave everyone a detention.

8. **Curdle** (v.): go bad or sour, turn from liquid to a solid mass, thicken, clot, congeal.
   Milk will <u>curdle</u> in warm weather and will have to be thrown out.

9. **Depression** (n.): state of deep unhappiness, despair, sadness; economic decline.
   After England's loss in the World Cup Semi-Finals, the national mood was one of <u>depression</u>.

10. **Affix** (v.): to fasten, attach, join.
    The landlord contracted builders to <u>affix</u> sprinklers to the ceiling, to protect the building in case of a fire.

Notes

Vocab 1
Cut-and-keep

feline

disgruntled

spurious

portray

secluded

nuptial

infuriate

curdle

depression

affix

Synonym Exercise A

Write the word from the vocab list which is most **similar** in meaning next to each word listed below.

1. Illustrate..
2. Congeal...
3. Fasten ....
4. Matrimonial..
5. Lonely...
6. Fake ....
7. Catlike...
8. Despair ....
9. Resentful ....
10. Enrage ....

Exercise B

Write the most suitable word from the vocab list in the spaces below. You might need to change the form of the word; for instance, walk might become walked.

1. The woman's piercing shriek made my blood ………………………………..
2. Little Red Riding Hood visited Grandma's ……………………………….. cottage in the depths of the wood.
3. The happy couple flew to Barbados to make their …………………………………vows on the beach.
4. The film Amadeus tries to ………………………………. the composer Salieri as a jealous, vicious man who causes Mozart's death.
5. The dancers moved with elegant, ………………………. grace across the wide stage.
6. In recent years, many mental health organisations have tried to raise greater awareness about ……………………………….
7. Elaine needed help to ………………………………. the camping badge to her scout uniform.
8. The boys' inappropriate behaviour began to ……………………………… their father, so he grounded them for two weeks.
9. The newspapers attacked the chief executive's …………………………… claims about his economic achievements.
10. John was ……………………………… when his boss yet again passed over him for promotion.

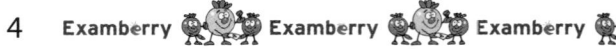

Exercise C

Select the most suitable word from the choice provided.

1. Queen Elizabeth I preferred artists to ………………………………. her as a beautiful young woman.
    - **a: portray**
    - **b: curdle**
    - **c: depression**

2. After the ……………………………. ceremony, the bride and groom left for their honeymoon.
    - **a: secluded**
    - **b: infuriate**
    - **c: nuptial**

3. The mysterious creature had an elongated body with large paws and a …………………. face.
    - **a: depression**
    - **b: affix**
    - **c: feline**

4. The Great …………………………….. ruined the American economy in the early 1930s and caused financial problems around the world.
    - **a: infuriate**
    - **b: depression**
    - **c: nuptial**

5. I knew my sister's cheeky comments would ………………………….. Dad, but as usual she could not keep quiet.
    - **a: spurious**
    - **b: infuriate**
    - **c: portray**

6. During the 19th century, panic about vampires caused even highly educated people to ………………………………. crucifixes and garlic to their doors as protection.
    - **a: affix**
    - **b: feline**
    - **c: curdle**

7. The hikers found a ………………………………. clearing in the forest in which to pitch their tents.
    - **a: disgruntled**
    - **b: spurious**
    - **c: secluded**

8. Custard will ……………………………. and become very lumpy if it is heated too quickly.
    - **a: curdle**
    - **b: nuptial**
    - **c: depression**

9. The businessman demanded an apology after he was wrongly jailed on ………………………………. corruption charges.
    - **a: spurious**
    - **b: affix**
    - **c: feline**

10. The restaurant manager calmed down the ……………………………. customer with a round of free drinks.
    - **a: disgruntled**
    - **b: depression**
    - **c: portray**

Vocab 1

Notes

Vocabulary 2

Learn the following words and then answer the questions.

1. **Rupture** (v.): rift, split, break, separation.

   The rusty old pipe <u>ruptured</u> at its weakest point causing water to flood the flat.

2. **Potter** (v.): to wander around, amuse oneself, loiter, dabble, tinker about.

   At the weekends, my dad would <u>potter</u> around the garden doing odd jobs.

3. **Aptitude** (n.): inclination, ability, propensity, knack, skill for.

   Vince has a natural <u>aptitude</u> for sports and is in many of the school teams.

4. **Conscientious** (adj.): thorough, careful; moral, principled, thoughtful.

   Ben was the most <u>conscientious</u> student, as he always completed his work on time and was respectful of his classmates.

5. **Manifest** (v.): to become visible, display, exhibit, reveal, appear.

   Having seen a dark shape <u>manifest</u> itself in the hallway, Eddy ran out of the house, afraid.

6. **Vain** (adj.): narcissistic, conceited, self-important, self-obsessed; futile, pointless, unsuccessful.

   The princess was so <u>vain</u> that she spent the entire day looking in the mirror.

7. **Diligence** (n.): perseverance, application, attentiveness.

   Mandip won the scholarship through sheer <u>diligence</u>, pushing herself to study every minute of the day.

8. **Heist** (n): robbery, raid, theft.

   Police have no suspects and few clues about the <u>heist</u> at the exclusive London jewellers.

9. **Taciturn** (adj.): reserved, uncommunicative, saying little, quiet.

   Although my grandfather was <u>taciturn</u> in large groups of people, he enjoyed talking to me on a one-to-one basis.

10. **Choreograph** (v.): compose a sequence of steps or moves (usually for a dance), plan and control.

    The new drama teacher's first task was to <u>choreograph</u> a dance for the Year 4 production.

Synonym Exercise A

Write the word from the vocab list which is most **similar** in meaning next to each word listed below.

1. Ability ....
2. Theft ....
3. Display ....
4. Careful ....
5. Plan ....
6. Uncommunicative ....
7. Self-important ....
8. Break ....
9. Loiter ....
10. Perseverance ....

Exercise B

Write the most suitable word from the vocab list in the spaces below. You might need to change the form of the word; for instance, walk might become walked.

1. The opening scene of the movie features the gangsters escaping the bank after a daring ....
2. Experts are concerned that use of social media is encouraging young people to be ....
3. The general began to .... a detailed battle plan involving thousands of soldiers.
4. The gardener was highly ...., keeping the flowerbeds neat and tidy, with not a weed in sight.
5. Grandma loved to .... around the house, rearranging books and ornaments.
6. Jane used to be .... as a child, but as she grew up she became more and more talkative.
7. Lizzy's .... for art meant that her drawings and paintings were always best in the class.
8. The dam wall began to .... soon after a small crack in the concrete was first spotted.
9. The Olympic rower said his success was due to a combination of .... and natural ability.
10. Belle continues to .... the same eagerness to read as when she picked up her very first book.

Vocab 2

Cut-and-keep

rupture

potter

aptitude

conscientious

manifest

vain

diligence

heist

taciturn

choreograph

Vocab 2

Exercise C

Select the most suitable word from the choice provided.

1. According to legend, Narcissus was so ………………………….. that he fell in love with his own reflection and was turned into a flower.

    a: rupture   **b: manifest**   **c: vain**

2. Relations between the two countries may ………………………………. entirely unless their presidents can come to an agreement soon.

    a: heist   **b: rupture**   **c: potter**

3. Billy was extremely outgoing and talkative, in complete contrast to his best friend Camilla, who was more introverted and …………………………….. .

    a: manifest   **b: taciturn**   **c: diligence**

4. Zofia was desperate for her……………………………. at work to be noticed, as she was hoping for a pay rise.

    a: diligence   **b: rupture**   **c: choreograph**

5. A ……………………….. student will complete and check through all their homework.

    a: aptitude   **b: conscientious**   **c: vain**

6. It is often a requirement to pass a test demonstrating natural ………………………….. before you are allowed to train as a doctor.

    a: aptitude   **b: diligence**   **c: rupture**

7. Susan ……………………………..ed around in the conservatory, watering the plants.

    a: manifest   **b: potter**   **c: heist**

8. The symptoms of the disease …………………………….ed themselves over a period of ten years, which made it far more difficult to detect.

    a: vain   **b: manifest**   **c: conscientious**

9. The young dancer ……………………………..ed the new ballet with very little assistance.

    a: potter   **b: taciturn**   **c: choreograph**

10. Chris pulled the train's alarm as soon as he realised the hooded men were planning a ……………………………….. .

    a: heist   **b: diligence**   **c: taciturn**

Vocabulary 3

Learn the following words and then answer the questions.

1. **Phenomenon** (n.): a rare occurrence or fact, wonder, marvel; an observable fact or event.

    In the 1980s and 1990s, the mysterious phenomenon of crop circles was first seen in the United States.

2. **Provoke** (v.): aggravate, start, incite, cause, goad.

    Dairy products may provoke allergic reactions in some people.

3. **Supremacy** (n.): total domination, control or power, leadership, influence.

    After their third goal, Manchester United's supremacy over Tottenham Hotspur was clearly established.

4. **Inventive** (adj.): creative, imaginative, resourceful.

    The movie was an inventive piece of film-making which the audience found fascinating.

5. **Perturb** (v.): upset, unsettle, disturb, ruffle.

    The sudden appearance of a bear did not perturb the wild rabbits in the slightest.

6. **Decisive** (adj.): definite, conclusive, crucial.

    William the Conqueror won a decisive victory at the Battle of Hastings that allowed him to claim the throne of England.

7. **Stability** (n.): the state of being stable or secure, strength, steadiness.

    The new government brought a sense of stability to the troubled country, after years of arguing over Brexit.

8. **Sanctuary** (n.): safe place (often religious), refuge, shelter, retreat.

    In recent years Borneo has invested a lot of money into building a new sanctuary for its endangered orangutans.

9. **Derive** (v.): to come from, originate, have origins in, evolve from.

    Many English words derive from Latin.

10. **Wildfire** (n.): a large fire that spreads rapidly over woodland or brush, and is difficult to extinguish, a blaze (used figuratively in reference to something spreading very quickly).

    Many of the forest animals were unable to escape the deadly wildfire which engulfed their habitats.

Notes

Vocab 3
Cut-and-keep

phenomenon

provoke

supremacy

inventive

perturb

decisive

stability

sanctuary

derive

wildfire

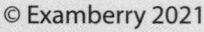

Synonym Exercise A

Write the word from the vocab list which is most **similar** in meaning next to each word listed below.

1. Domination ....
2. Steadiness ....
3. Goad ....
4. Conclusive ....
5. Blaze ....
6. Creative ....
7. Wonder ....
8. Originate ....
9. Unsettle ....
10. Shelter ....

Exercise B

Write the most suitable word from the vocab list in the spaces below. You might need to change the form of the word; for instance, walk might become walked.

1. Mozart was considered a .... because he could play the piano brilliantly at only four years old.

2. The cloaked man's sinister stare began to .... me as I realised he was following us home.

3. Lynne hopes her article will .... readers into thinking seriously about the issue.

4. The news of Jessica's success at school spread like .... through her hometown.

5. The Bank of England's new policy brought greater financial .... to many households across the country.

6. During the Medieval period, people were able to seek .... in churches and remain there safely there for up to fifty days.

7. The Harry Potter books are essentially about the fight for .... between the forces of good and evil.

8. Fortunately, Jane's fertile and ....…..... imagination came to her aid during her creative writing task.

9. The manager's advice was the .... factor in the rugby team's triumph at the World Cup.

10. Much of the book's appeal seems to .... from the endearing personality of the central character.

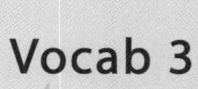

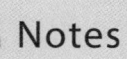

Exercise C

Select the most suitable word from the choice provided.

1. Polly's constant lateness began to .... her mother, who was always on time.

    a: perturb   **b: inventive**   **c: derive**

2. The bridge's strength and .... was such that even heavy tractors and lorries could drive across it.

    a: decisive   **b: stability**   **c: wildfire**

3. Kate was delighted that her .... design for the school's new logo won first prize in the competition.

    a: sanctuary   **b: inventive**   **c: provoke**

4. Bullies often try to .... a reaction from their victims to get them into trouble.

    a: provoke   **b: phenomenon**   **c: perturb**

5. Meerkats............................. great benefit from living in groups, as this allows the sharing of food and gives protection from birds of prey.

    a: stability   **b: wildfire**   **c: derive**

6. The recent Californian ....s were the deadliest on record, killing around fifty people and devastating many acres of woodland.

    a: phenomenon   **b: wildfire**   **c: inventive**

7. Great leaders are not necessarily always right, but they are often .... at crucial moments.

    a: sanctuary   **b: perturb**   **c: decisive**

8. Kamran was thrilled to see the unique natural .... of the Northern Lights on his recent school trip to Iceland.

    a: phenomenon   **b: wildfire**   **c: inventive**

9. Animal charities have set up wildlife .... across the globe to protect endangered species.

    a: derive   **b: sanctuaries**   **c: stability**

10. The huge gorilla quickly established .... over the rest of the troop.

    a: perturb   **b: stability**   **c: supremacy**

Vocabulary 4

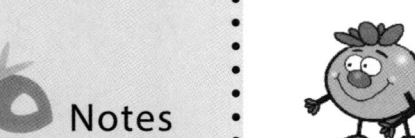

Learn the following words and then answer the questions.

1. **Dweller** (n.): inhabitant, resident, occupant.

   Both city and country <u>dwellers</u> should pay taxes for services like the NHS.

2. **Cautious** (adj.): careful, aware, vigilant, wary.

   It is important to be <u>cautious</u> when crossing a road, even on a zebra crossing.

3. **Imply** (v.): suggest, mean, indicate, hint.

   Just because I suggested eating out, that does not <u>imply</u> that I am fed up with your cooking!

4. **Deduct** (v.): take, remove, subtract.

   The teacher threatened to <u>deduct</u> marks from the essay if it was handed in late.

5. **Detest** (v.): hate, loathe, despise.

   I <u>detest</u> spending money unnecessarily, so I take my own packed lunch to school rather than buy it in the canteen.

6. **Broadcast** (v.): to transmit, make public, send out, show, advertise.

   Every Sunday at 8pm, Channel 4 <u>broadcasts</u> my favourite television programme.

7. **Henceforth** (adv.): from now on, in future.

   '<u>Henceforth</u>, I expect you to be punctual for meetings,' my boss snapped at me as I walked in 10 minutes late.

8. **Retail** (adj.): connected with selling of goods to the public for consumption or use, shopping.

   The cake business has fifteen <u>retail</u> shops in Hampshire alone.

9. **Hallmark** (n.): a distinctive characteristic or attribute; a mark on an article to indicate its authenticity, guarantee, stamp, symbol.

   Attention to detail is the <u>hallmark</u> of a fine craftsman.

10. **Common sense** (n.): intelligence, good sense, sound judgement.

    It is <u>common sense</u> to carry an umbrella in wet weather.

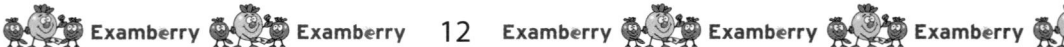

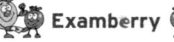

Vocab 4
Cut-and-keep

dweller

cautious

imply

deduct

detest

broadcast

henceforth

retail

hallmark

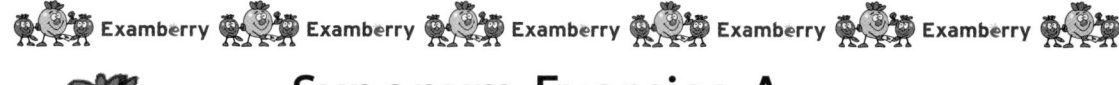

common sense

Synonym Exercise A

Write the word from the vocab list which is most **similar** in meaning next to each word listed below.

1. In future ....
2. Hate ....
3. Wary ....
4. Symbol ....
5. Hint ....
6. Intelligence ....
7. Transmit ....
8. Subtract ....
9. Resident ....
10. Shopping ....

Exercise B

Write the most suitable word from the vocab list in the spaces below. You might need to change the form of the word; for instance, walk might become walked.

1. During a driving test, examiners ………………………………. marks for every mistake, no matter how small.

2. Amber advised me to be ……………………………….. when I opened the tank to feed the frogs, in case one jumped out.

3. The ………………………………. of the director Steven Spielberg's films are the magnificent special effects.

4. It is ………………………………. to keep all medicines out of reach of children.

5. During the radio interview, the politician …………………………. her intention to run for Prime Minister to millions of listeners.

6. To a city ……………………………….., the silence of the countryside can be eerie.

7. Ted's baffled look seemed to ………………………………. that he did not understand the question.

8. Jeremiah Sidebottom-Smith decided to change his name, and said that ………………………………. he would simply be known as Jerry Smith.

9. I absolutely ……………………………. cauliflower, unless it is covered in cheese sauce.

10. The record profits in the ………………………………. sales sector indicate a boom in the economy.

Vocab 4 Notes

Exercise C

Select the most suitable word from the choice provided.

1. Gold, silver and platinum jewellery must be stamped with a special ……………………….. to certify its purity.

    a: hallmark   b: deduct   c: cautious

2. The only ……………………..…. in the tiny cottage was an elderly farmer.

    a: imply   b: henceforth   c: dweller

3. The footballer was told that his club would ………………………………. a week's salary as punishment for his bad behaviour.

    a: deduct   b: common sense   c: retail

4. Many people loathe and ……………………….. rats, even though they have never even seen one.

    a: henceforth   b: detest   c: broadcast

5. "How dare you ………………………….. that I am lying," yelled my little sister angrily.

    a: dweller   b: cautious   c: imply

6. The boys showed a distinct lack of ………………………….. by trying to jump over a spiked fence to outrun the police.

    a: retail   b: common sense   c: hallmark

7. For her New Year's resolution, Amy declared that …...…………………….. she would tidy her room and make her bed every day.

    a: henceforth   b: hallmark   c: deduct

8. Paul failed to be ……………………..……………. while driving on the wet road and crashed into a lamp-post.

    a: imply   b: cautious   c: common sense

9. The programme will be ……………………….. with subtitles for the hard of hearing.

    a: cautious   b: detest   c: broadcast

10. The shopkeeper bought a selection of trousers at a bargain price, which was well below the ……………………………. value.

    a: retail   b: deduct   c: hallmark

Vocabulary 5

Learn the following words and then answer the questions.

1. **Exemplify** (v.): to show by example, demonstrate, depict.

   Children who exemplify both a good work ethic and a friendly attitude may be chosen as school prefects.

2. **Punctual** (adj.): being on time, prompt, on schedule.

   Lucy was always punctual and she disliked the fact that her friends were usually late when they met at the park.

3. **Encounter** (v.): to come across something or someone without warning, meet, run into.

   I never thought I would encounter a snake in my garden in West London.

4. **Roam** (v.): to wander, travel, journey.

   Nick allowed his dogs to roam free in the field, but put them on leads when they approached the road.

5. **Concave** (adj.): curved, depressed, dented, a surface that curves inwards like the interior of a sphere.

   By sitting up straight in your chair, you will help to support your lower back curve, which is concave.

6. **Ornamental** (adj.): decorative, ornate, attractive, for show.

   The pillars in the centre of the room are purely ornamental; they look elegant but do not help support the ceiling.

7. **Abysmal** (adj.): terrible, awful, appalling, dreadful.

   The living conditions in Victorian Britain were abysmal for the poor, especially in urban slums.

8. **Catapult** (v.): hurl, throw, toss, fling.

   When the alarm clock goes off, I catapult myself out of bed and get ready for school.

9. **Venture** (n.): an undertaking, enterprise, gamble, mission, activity.

   Any business venture usually involves an element of risk, so investors may make a profit or lose all their money.

10. **Enact** (v.): to pass into law, approve, validate, put into practice; act out eg. on stage.

    The government has failed so far to enact a law allowing students to attend university free of charge.

Notes

Vocab 5
Cut-and-keep

- exemplify
- punctual
- encounter
- roam
- concave
- ornamental
- abysmal
- catapult
- venture
- enact

Synonym Exercise A

Write the word from the vocab list which is most **similar** in meaning next to each word listed below.

1. Wander..
2. Dreadful ....
3. Prompt ....
4. Approve ....
5. Demonstrate..
6. Enterprise..
7. Meet...
8. Decorative...
9. Curved...
10. Fling ....

Exercise B

Write the most suitable word from the vocab list in the spaces below. You might need to change the form of the word; for instance, walk might become walked.

1. The Romans used wooden machinery to ………………………….. huge rocks at the enemy wall.

2. Su-Lin won the school prize as her kindly nature was seen to …………………………. the school's values of citizenship and decency.

3. Many of Shakespeare's plays were first ……………………………ed in the original Globe Theatre.

4. We were told that the school trip would depart promptly at 8:30am, and that if we were not ……………………………….., we would be left behind!

5. Lily's ice cream business will only be a profitable ………………………… in the summer holidays.

6. The plant's attractive purple berries were not edible, but purely ………………………..

7. Kate hoped she would ………………………….. many famous celebrities on her trip to Hollywood.

8. The teacher told Alex that his essay was the most ………………………….. piece of writing that she had ever had the misfortune to read.

9. Many flowers have five petals, usually ………………………….. or spoon-shaped.

10. The children were allowed to …………………………… freely around the castle, exploring it in their own time.

Exercise C

Select the most suitable word from the choice provided.

1. It is important to be ……………………………….. when you attend a job interview, as being late does not make a good first impression!

    a: exemplify   **b: punctual**   **c: venture**

2. In the Hall of Mirrors, we saw hilarious, distorted images of ourselves in the convex and ………………………………. glass panels.

    a: concave   **b: encounter**   **c: roam**

3. Public opinion forced Parliament to ………………………………. a new law banning smoking in restaurants.

    a: catapult   **b: ornamental**   **c: enact**

4. The physics teacher drew a diagram to ……………………………….. the theory of magnetic fields.

    a: abysmal   **b: exemplify**   **c: encounter**

5. MI6 sent their best spy on a daring ………………………………. to prevent the murder of a famous politician in Mozambique.

    a: venture   **b: concave**   **c: exemplify**

6. The stream flowed into several ……………………………. lakes in the vast gardens of the estate.

    a: roam   **b: punctual**   **c: ornamental**

7. Roger Federer's victory in the Wimbledon finals ……………………………….ed him up the world rankings into second place.

    a: ornamental   **b: catapult**   **c: concave**

8. Sherlock Holmes was unsure who he would ………………………………. in the sinister mansion.

    a: venture   **b: abysmal**   **c: encounter**

9. Gareth was dropped from the rugby team following his numerous ……………………… performances throughout the season.

    a: exemplify   **b: abysmal**   **c: punctual**

10. Our neighbour keeps chickens, which ………………………………. freely around her garden.

    a: catapult   **b: roam**   **c: exemplify**

Vocab 5

Notes

Vocabulary 6

Learn the following words and then answer the questions.

1. **Convex** (adj.): a surface that curves outward, like the exterior of a sphere, protuberant, arched, bulging.

    Eyeballs are <u>convex</u> in shape.

2. **Unbelievable** (adj.): astonishing, beyond the imagination, incredible, impossible.

    Emma's suggestion that the dog ate her homework was <u>unbelievable</u> and the teacher told her off for lying.

3. **Continuation** (n.): addition, extension, preservation.

    The new book is a <u>continuation</u> of the author's autobiography and details her later life.

4. **Antidote** (n.): anything that will counteract the effects of poison or disease, cure, remedy.

    The doctor knew he would have to administer the <u>antidote</u> within an hour to save Paul from the venomous snake bite.

5. **Epiphany** (n.): a revelation, inspiration, moment of sudden realisation.

    I felt my moment of <u>epiphany</u> had come as suddenly I realised I should train as a doctor.

6. **Wither** (v.): weaken, fade, decline, shrivel.

    Flowers can quickly <u>wither</u> and die if you do not water them during the hot summer days.

7. **Opulent** (adj.): rich, luxurious, deluxe.

    The wealthy businessman lived in a mansion decorated in an <u>opulent</u> style, with marble and gold throughout.

8. **Literary** (adj.): concerning the writing, study, or content of literature, well-read, scholarly.

    Charles Dickens's novel Great Expectations is among the great <u>literary</u> works of the 19th century.

9. **Avenge** (v.): retaliate, punish, take revenge.

    The footballers wanted to <u>avenge</u> their humiliating defeat of the previous year, when they were beaten by six goals to nil.

10. **Donor** (n.): a person who gives something (especially to charities), patron, benefactor.

    Hospitals encourage people to become blood <u>donors</u> so that they can save lives using blood transfusions.

Vocab 6 — Cut-and-keep

convex
unbelievable
continuation
antidote
epiphany
wither
opulent
literary
avenge
donor

Synonym Exercise A

Write the word from the vocab list which is most **similar** in meaning next to each word listed below.

1. Incredible ....
2. Extension ....
3. Shrivel ....
4. Retaliate ....
5. Patron ....
6. Cure ....
7. Bulging ....
8. Revelation ....
9. Luxurious ....
10. Scholarly ....

Exercise B

Write the most suitable word from the vocab list in the spaces below. You might need to change the form of the word; for instance, walk might become walked.

1. The proposed new road will be a ………………………….. of the M1 motorway.
2. The gardener sprayed weed-killer on the lawn and after only an hour the dandelions began to …………………………..
3. The Booker Prize is an annual ………………………….. award for the best novel written in the English language.
4. In a tennis match of ………………………….. excitement and drama, the world champion was beaten by a 16-year-old newcomer.
5. The famous actress liked to travel in an ………………………….. style, using limousines and private jets.
6. Harry Potter swore that he would ………………………….. his parents' deaths.
7. Doing sports at school can be a good ………………………….. to the stress of exams.
8. An anonymous ………………………….. gave a million pounds to the animal charity.
9. Many cars have ………………………….. wing mirrors, which give drivers a wider field of vision behind them.
10. The famous ancient physicist, Archimedes, was said to have had an ………………………….. in the bath, shouting 'Eureka' when he realised that his body displaced the water.

Vocab 6

Exercise C

Select the most suitable word from the choice provided.

1. Lucy is waiting for a new kidney from an organ ………………………….. but it may take years before one is found.

    a: unbelievable   b: donor   c: epiphany

2. Everyone in the class thought Mia's low score in the maths test was …………………….. as usually she came top.

    a: opulent   b: continuation   c: unbelievable

3. It is important to read ………………………………….. works from countries around the world to be able to appreciate different cultures and societies.

    a: literary   b: avenge   c: convex

4. Apples left in the fruit bowl for months will start to …………………………….. and eventually shrivel up completely.

    a: antidote   b: wither   c: opulent

5. The farmer plotted to ………………………..………. the illegal slaughter of his sheep by his rival across the valley.

    a: wither   b: donor   c: avenge

6. An ice cream scoop's ……………………………. shape makes it ideal for producing perfect round portions.

    a: convex   b: continuation   c: literary

7. The …………………………………. of the strike for another week caused the government to lose hundreds of thousands of pounds.

    a: avenge   b: continuation   c: antidote

8. The golden throne was an …………………………………… reminder of the king's wealth.

    a: continuation   b: unbelievable   c: opulent

9. Saul had an ………………………………… on the road to Damascus; he changed his name to Paul, and became a Christian.

    a: opulent   b: epiphany   c: wither

10. The only …………………………. to the poisonous mushroom was a fluid secreted by a female frog.

    a: antidote   b: donor   c: unbelievable

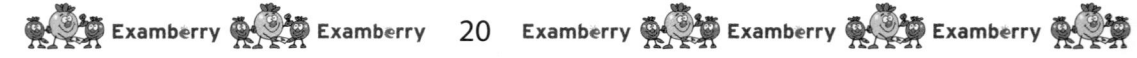

Vocabulary 7

Learn the following words and then answer the questions.

1. **Scruple** (n.): (usually plural - scruples) ethical or moral doubt, pang of conscience, hesitation, qualm(s).

   The boy had no scruples about cheating in his exams as he did not think it mattered.

2. **Equality** (n.): fairness, balance, the state of being equal (especially in status, rights or opportunities).

   Companies have a duty to eliminate discrimination and promote gender equality.

3. **Garnish** (v.): decorate, embellish, top (especially with food).

   When I cook fajitas, I like to garnish each serving with a dollop of sour cream or salsa.

4. **Anatomy** (n.): structure, makeup, framework, body of an organism.

   In the Biology lesson, we dissected a frog to study its anatomy in great detail.

5. **Mourn** (v.): to feel deep sadness after the death of a loved one, grieve, lament.

   On Remembrance Sunday, we mourn the loss of all those who died fighting for our country in war.

6. **Hygienic** (adj.): clean, sterile, healthy.

   An inspector ensures that the school lunches are prepared in hygienic conditions to prevent outbreaks of food poisoning.

7. **Institution** (n.): an organisation founded for a religious, educational, professional or social purpose; academy, establishment.

   The health and wellbeing institution was built to help those with long-term mental illnesses.

8. **Lapel** (n.): the fold at the front of a coat or jacket, continuation of the coat collar.

   A flower was pinned to the lapel of Jake's jacket on his wedding day.

9. **Congregate** (v.): assemble, flock, converge, gather.

   The students were asked to congregate in the assembly hall every Monday morning to hear the headteacher's address.

10. **Discontinued** (adj.): cancelled, finished, withdrawn, ended.

    The bus service in Edinburgh was discontinued because nobody used it after the tram was introduced.

Notes

Vocab 7
Cut-and-keep

- scruple
- equality
- garnish
- anatomy
- mourn
- hygienic
- institution
- lapel
- congregate
- discontinued

Synonym Exercise A

Write the word from the vocab list which is most **similar** in meaning next to each word listed below.

1. Hesitation..
2. Gather..
3. Sterile..
4. Embellish...
5. Ended..
6. Establishment..
7. Structure...
8. Fairness..
9. Grieve...
10. Collar...

Exercise B

Write the most suitable word from the vocab list in the spaces below. You might need to change the form of the word; for instance, walk might become walked.

1. The Suffragettes demanded ………………………… and the right to vote in elections in the early 20th century.

2. The surgeon put on a new, ………………………….. medical suit before carrying out every operation.

3. Fresh herbs can be used to …………………………. an otherwise dull looking dish.

4. After the invention of the microscope, our knowledge of plant …………………..……….. greatly improved.

5. The wine stained the ……………………….. of Sophia's white jacket after the waiter tripped and dropped the open bottle.

6. Jess's selfish brother had no ……………………….s about eating all the chocolate biscuits.

7. The old school uniform was ……………………………. and a completely new style introduced.

8. Thousands of people …………………………….d in front of the stage waiting for Ed Sheeran to come on.

9. Many churches held services to ………………………… the victims of the devastating fire.

10. The teenagers who carried out the robbery were sent to a Young Offenders' ………………………. for six months.

Exercise C

Select the most suitable word from the choice provided.

1. The elephant …………………………….ed the loss of her calf who was sadly killed by a hunter.

    a: mourn　　　**b: scruple**　　　**c: anatomy**

2. The roast potatoes were …………………………….ed with a dollop of mayonnaise and a sprinkling of paprika.

    a: garnish　　　**b: mourn**　　　**c: institution**

3. Jack had no …………………………….s about cheating his grandmother out of all her savings.

    a: discontinued　　　**b: lapel**　　　**c: scruple**

4. The diamond brooch pinned to Meryl's …………………………. sparkled when it caught the light.

    a: lapel　　　**b: congregate**　　　**c: garnish**

5. The dentist's tools had to be ……………..…………… and sterile, otherwise they could spread infection.

    a: scruple　　　**b: equality**　　　**c: hygienic**

6. The passengers …………………………….d on the upper deck of the boat to hear the talk on marine life.

    a: institution　　　**b: congregate**　　　**c: anatomy**

7. We must strive for …………………………. between men and women across the globe.

    a: garnish　　　**b: lapel**　　　**c: equality**

8. Amanda's gym membership was automatically …………………………. as she had forgotten to pay the fees.

    a: discontinued　　　**b: anatomy**　　　**c: congregate**

9. The medical students began to study the complexities of human ……………………….

    a: scruple　　　**b: anatomy**　　　**c: hygienic**

10. The scientific ……………………………….. gave advice to schools on various aspects of chemistry and biology.

    a: lapel　　　**b: equality**　　　**c: institution**

Vocab 7

Notes

Vocabulary 8

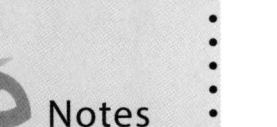

Learn the following words and then answer the questions.

1. **Analyst** (n.): a person who inspects and looks closely at something, an investigator, predictor, specialist.

   My financial <u>analyst</u> studied the market and recommended the best bank account for me.

2. **Divinity** (n.): theology, the quality or character of being godlike, divine being, holiness.

   Christians believe in the <u>divinity</u> of Jesus Christ.

3. **Averse** (adj.): reluctant, opposing, unwilling.

   For those who are <u>averse</u> to eating meat, there is also a vegetarian option.

4. **Forte** (n.): a strong point, an area in which an individual excels, skill, talent.

   John knew comedy was not his <u>forte</u> when he failed to get a single laugh from the friendly audience.

5. **Befriend** (v.): to make friends with; look after, protect.

   The quickest way to <u>befriend</u> someone is just to smile and chat in a relaxed way.

6. **Lukewarm** (adj.): moderately warm, feeling or showing little interest or enthusiasm, tepid.

   I thought my idea for the project was brilliant but it only received <u>lukewarm</u> support from my classmates.

7. **Demeanour** (n.): attitude, manner, behaviour, presence.

   Freddie's disruptive <u>demeanour</u> resulted in his suspension from school for a week.

8. **Morgue** (n.): mortuary, undertaker's, a building where dead bodies are kept before burial or cremation.

   The witness had to go to the <u>morgue</u> to identify the victim's body.

9. **Dominance** (n.): having power over, supremacy, control.

   In his time, the French Emperor Napoleon achieved <u>dominance</u> over the European continent.

10. **Slander** (n.): a false and malicious statement against someone, which is damaging to their reputation, slur.

    The politician sued a newspaper for <u>slander</u> after it suggested, without any evidence, that she had received bribes.

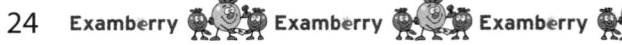

Vocab 8

Cut-and-keep

analyst
divinity
averse
forte
befriend
lukewarm
demeanour
morgue
dominance
slander

Synonym Exercise A

Write the word from the vocab list which is most **similar** in meaning next to each word listed below.

1. Talent ....
2. Tepid ....
3. Control ....
4. Holiness ....
5. Mortuary ....
6. Make friends with ....
7. Behaviour ....
8. Slur ....
9. Unwilling ....
10. Investigator ....

Exercise B

Write the most suitable word from the vocab list in the spaces below. You might need to change the form of the word; for instance, walk might become walked.

1. Olivia's happy .... masked her disappointment with her latest grades.
2. Both leaders were strongly .... to war, and solved their differences by talking instead.
3. Laws against .... are used to punish unacceptable speech.
4. The teacher suggested to Alice that she make an effort to .... a new student who had just joined the class.
5. Roman .... over Britain was finally achieved by the Emperor Claudius in 43 CE.
6. After the shoot-out, the .... was full of the rival gangsters' dead bodies.
7. Barney found that rugby was his .... after he excelled in a trial session at a local club.
8. The handwriting .... could describe a person's character just by studying their writing.
9. Ali complained to the waiter that his soup was only .... rather than piping hot.
10. Unlike most modern religions, the Ancient Greeks believed in many gods and not just in a single ....

Exercise C

Select the most suitable word from the choice provided.

1. Lucy maintained a calm ………………………….. throughout her interview at the secondary school, which impressed the Headmaster.

    a: divinity **b: analyst** **c: demeanour**

2. The crowd could see that juggling was clearly not the clown's ………………………….., after he dropped the balls several times.

    a: lukewarm **b: forte** **c: befriend**

3. The president was accused of …………………………. after he announced that his rival had not paid his taxes.

    a: analyst **b: slander** **c: morgue**

4. The film received only …………………………. reviews from the critics, who stated that the special effects were poor and the acting dreadful.

    a: averse **b: dominance** **c: lukewarm**

5. Detectives spent hours examining the corpse in the ……………………. before the murder trial.

    a: slander **b: morgue** **c: divinity**

6. The teacher told Oliver's parents that he was …………………………. to hard work and had not handed in most of the term's homework.

    a: averse **b: forte** **c: lukewarm**

7. The football coach was a shrewd ………………………….. of the opposition players' strengths and weaknesses.

    a: demeanour **b: befriend** **c: analyst**

8. Leigh ……………………………..ed the homeless boy, offering him food and a place to sleep.

    a: befriend **b: lukewarm** **c: morgue**

9. The toy manufacturer was able to achieve complete …………………………. over its competitors in the run-up to Christmas.

    a: averse **b: dominance** **c: slander**

10. In ancient China, a mountain was seen as a ………………………… with the power to send rain.

    a: divinity **b: morgue** **c: demeanour**

Vocabulary 9

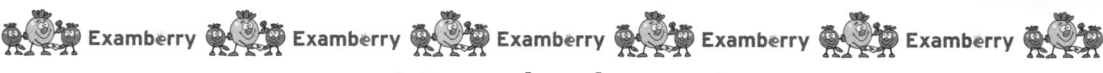

Learn the following words and then answer the questions.

1. **Profuse** (adj.): excessive, abundant, copious.

   Profuse amounts of grey hair sprouted from Granddad's bushy eyebrows.

2. **Abide** (v.): submit to, put up with, tolerate, accept.

   Although Ellie despises the school uniform, she must abide by the rules and wear it every day.

3. **Complement** (n.): a number or quantity required to make a group complete, counterpart, accompaniment, match.

   When working on the drama project, Jim was the perfect complement to Ariana as he was methodical and she was imaginative.

4. **Seldom** (adv.): not often, rarely, infrequently.

   Laura seldom eats chocolate, but on rare occasions she has a Kit Kat and savours every bite!

5. **Fellowship** (n.): friendship, partnership, companionship, group.

   Steve enjoyed the fellowship of other actors in the company, after the loneliness of his solo tour.

6. **Anticipation** (n.): expectation, hope, awareness, readiness.

   The audience members held their breath in anticipation before Beyoncé started singing her most famous hit.

7. **Expose** (v.): reveal, bring to light, endanger.

   The newspaper published an article which exposed the famous businessman as a fraud and a liar.

8. **Mayhem** (n.): extreme disorder, chaos, turmoil, anarchy.

   There was mayhem when everyone tried to flee at once after the fire alarm sounded.

9. **Prosperous** (adj.): well off, wealthy, successful.

   Farmers were more prosperous in the south of the country due to the fertile land which produced many crops.

10. **Dowry** (n.): the property, possessions or money that wives traditionally gave their husbands upon marriage, gift.

    When my grandparents married, my grandmother's dowry included a flock of sheep.

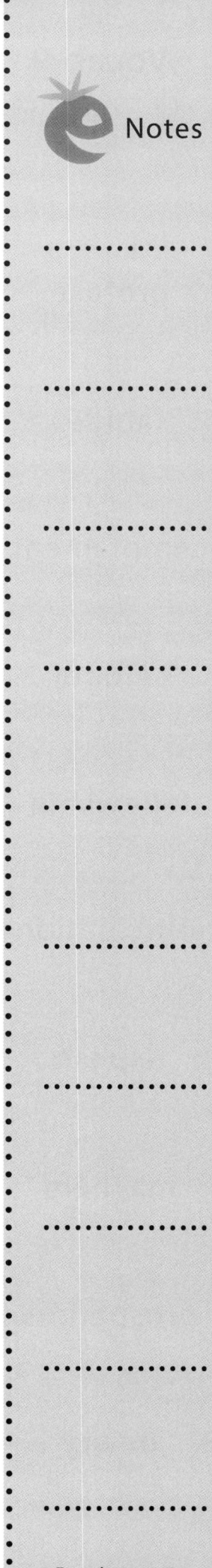

Notes

Vocab 9
Cut-and-keep

profuse

abide

complement

seldom

fellowship

anticipation

expose

mayhem

prosperous

dowry

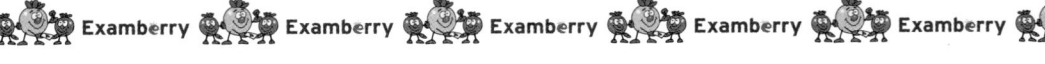

Synonym Exercise A
Write the word from the vocab list which is most **similar** in meaning next to each word listed below.

1. Rarely ....
2. Reveal ....
3. Counterpart ....
4. Wealthy ....
5. Gift ....
6. Excessive ....
7. Chaos ....
8. Tolerate ....
9. Partnership ....
10. Expectation ....

Exercise B
Write the most suitable word from the vocab list in the spaces below. You might need to change the form of the word; for instance, walk might become walked.

1. The ………………………. chef had made money writing and selling cookbooks.

2. James was very shy, and felt uncomfortable at the ……………………….. amounts of praise he received as the school essay prize winner.

3. Anya chose a new paint colour for the walls as a ……………………. to her dark brown carpet.

4. After the snow fell, the children created ………………………………. in the playground by throwing snowballs and sliding on the ice.

5. Camels have evolved to conserve water in their humps because it ………………..……… rains in the desert.

6. In the medieval period, princes would often marry for the sake of their wife's ………………………….. , to extend their lands and influence.

7. At the TV fundraising event, the phone-lines were manned in …………………………. of a flood of callers.

8. I cannot ……………………………. people who are constantly late.

9. A special ………………………….. was created between the schoolgirls when they realised how much they had in common.

10. I am always very careful not to ……………………………. my skin to the sun for too long to avoid sunburn.

Exercise C

Select the most suitable word from the choice provided.

1. Liam offered …………….………….. apologies for arriving so late at the birthday party.

    a: profuse **b: seldom** **c: anticipation**

2. I was not accepted as a volunteer this Christmas because the charity's …….…..………….. was already full.

    a: dowry **b: expose** **c: complement**

3. Princess Anastasia hoped that no one would ……………………………… her true identity: her royal status would endanger her life.

    a: profuse **b: abide** **c: expose**

4. It was utter ……………………………. at the restaurant last Friday when the manager did not turn up.

    a: mayhem **b: anticipation** **c: seldom**

5. People are stocking up on food at the supermarket in …………………….....…..……. of storms and flooding.

    a: profuse **b: anticipation** **c: expose**

6. "This is my house now and you will …………….....………….. by my rules!" shouted the wicked step-mother.

    a: fellowship **b: complement** **c: abide**

7. There was a strong feeling of ……………………………...……... amongst members of the hockey team after their overseas tour.

    a: fellowship **b: dowry** **c: abide**

8. I …………....……………………… go to the cinema because I prefer to watch films on DVD or Netflix at home.

    a: seldom **b: mayhem** **c: anticipation**

9. The business became more ……………………………... after it started to advertise online.

    a: complement **b: abide** **c: prosperous**

10. In some cultures, the tradition of a ………………….....………. persists, making marriage difficult for poorer women.

    a: dowry **b: expose** **c: profuse**

Vocab 9

Notes

Vocabulary 10

Learn the following words and then answer the questions.

1. **Rational** (adj.): sensible, logical, having the ability to reason or use common sense.

    Sherlock Holmes was known for his clear and rational analysis of a crime scene.

2. **Estrange** (v.): to alienate, drive away, put at a distance, divorce.

    Bob's bad temper served to estrange him from his family members, as they could no longer tolerate his rages.

3. **Vault** (n.): cellar, tomb, underground storage chamber, secure room.

    Archaeologists stumbled upon an underground vault filled with gold and other valuables.

4. **Vivacious** (adj.): cheerful, lively, spirited.

    Bill's cousin is vivacious and always very amusing to chat to.

5. **Rescind** (v.): abolish, annul, withdraw, declare null and void.

    The President's outrageous comments caused many people to rescind their support for him and vote for the opposition.

6. **Degrade** (v.): reduce, shame, humiliate, demean.

    The Head Teacher reminded the students that they must not degrade the school's reputation with poor behaviour.

7. **Establish** (v.): to create or form, start, launch, begin.

    During the rugby tour to New Zealand, the students established a strong link with their host schools.

8. **Predator** (n.): hunter, killer, an animal that naturally preys on others, a person who ruthlessly exploits others.

    The polar bear is the most dangerous predator in the Arctic and mainly preys on seals.

9. **Advent** (n.): beginning, arrival, onset; period leading to Christmas (proper noun so this meaning requires a capital).

    With the advent of the Internet, working from home has become common practice.

10. **Imaginative** (adj.): creative, inventive, ingenious.

    Eleanor's imaginative design and talent for painting meant that she was certain to win the school art competition.

Synonym Exercise A

Write the word from the vocab list which is most **similar** in meaning next to each word listed below.

1. Launch..
2. Arrival..
3. Logical..
4. Inventive..
5. Cellar..
6. Withdraw...
7. Divorce...
8. Demean..
9. Lively..
10. Hunter..

Exercise B

Write the most suitable word from the vocab list in the spaces below. You might need to change the form of the word; for instance, walk might become walked.

1. According to legend, Romulus and Remus ………………………………….ed the city of Rome in 753 BCE.

2. Julie came up with an ……………………………….. solution to the problem, when no one else in the class had any ideas.

3. The ………………………………. child made friends quickly due to her lively, friendly nature.

4. I cannot have a ……………………………….. discussion with my confused uncle.

5. The prince was …………………………..d from his family when he married a peasant girl instead of the princess he was promised to.

6. The judge said Joseph was an evil ……………..……………..……… who had tricked vulnerable people out of their savings.

7. The Pharaoh wished to be buried in the family ………………………………. alongside many of his ancient relatives.

8. Some foodstuffs begin to ……………………………….. in quality when exposed to air and heat.

9. Mum said she would ……………………..………… her offer of a £10 payment for washing the car unless I did it straight away.

10. Feather quills were the chief writing implement until the …………………………….. of steel pens in the nineteenth century.

Vocab 10

Cut-and-keep

- rational
- estrange
- vault
- vivacious
- rescind
- degrade
- establish
- predator
- advent
- imaginative

Exercise C

Select the most suitable word from the choice provided.

1. There was no ………………………………. explanation for Hassan's bizarre behaviour.

    a: rational   b: rescind   c: advent

2. Fraser's mother bought him a chocolate-filled calendar for ……………………….., with a window to open on each day of December up until Christmas.

    a: establish   b: rational   c: advent

3. Arlene won the Creative Writing Prize for her …………………………… and unusual story.

    a: imaginative   b: estrange   c: vault

4. The great white shark is the ocean's most fearsome ……………………………….

    a: advent   b: predator   c: rescind

5. High levels of pollution have ………………………....…….d the air quality in many cities.

    a: degrade   b: imaginative   c: vault

6. My uncle was ……………………….……..d from my father after an argument about who should run the family business.

    a: vivacious   b: estrange   c: predator

7. Benji bounded around the room energetically, true to his …………………….………. nature.

    a: vivacious   b: predator   c: rational

8. The Bank of England was first …………………………..…….ed in July 1694.

    a: rescind   b: establish   c: vivacious

9. The television replay showed that the footballer had been fouled, and so the red card he had been given was …………………………..……..……...ed.

    a: rescind   b: advent   c: predator

10. The Lestrange family …………………………… was located at Gringotts Wizarding Bank.

    a: heist   b: rupture   c: vault

Vocabulary 11

Learn the following words and then answer the questions.

1. **Confess** (v.): admit, own up, acknowledge, reveal.

   I must confess that, much to my shame, I have only ever watched the Harry Potter films and not read the books.

2. **Eloquent** (adj.): fluent, clear or impressive in speech or writing, articulate.

   Henry gave an eloquent speech to the whole school about his trip to Africa, with vivid descriptions of the animals he had seen.

3. **Bewildered** (adj.): confused, puzzled, baffled.

   The driver was bewildered by conflicting road signs and quickly became lost.

4. **Generation** (n.): age group, peer group, cohort.

   My grandparents' generation is not used to new technology and so I have to help them with sending emails.

5. **Odour** (n.): (usually unpleasant) smell, scent, fragrance.

   The chef was aware of the unpleasant odour coming from the burning cooking oil.

6. **Briskly** (adv.): quickly, energetically, hurriedly, rapidly.

   Pablo walked briskly through the park, trying to keep up with his dog.

7. **Refine** (v.): to improve or make better, enhance, upgrade.

   The musician took time to refine and improve her songs before putting them out on YouTube.

8. **Aggravate** (v.): to make worse, annoy, irritate.

   Scratching a mosquito bite can aggravate the pain and make the inflammation worse.

9. **Decrepit** (adj.): deteriorated, broken-down, rickety, derelict.

   It was sad that the famous medieval castle had been left to fall into such a decrepit state.

10. **Charcoal** (n.): a black solid obtained by heating organic matter in the absence of air, a stick of black carbon used for drawing.

    We used charcoal as fuel for our barbeque to grill the sausages and chicken.

Notes

Vocab 11
Cut-and-keep

- confess
- eloquent
- bewildered
- generation
- odour
- briskly
- refine
- aggravate
- decrepit
- charcoal

Synonym Exercise A

Write the word from the vocab list which is most **similar** in meaning next to each word listed below.

1. Irritate ....
2. Cohort ....
3. Rickety ....
4. Rapidly ....
5. Scent ....
6. Improve ....
7. Puzzled ....
8. Articulate ....
9. Carbon ....
10. Admit ....

Exercise B

Write the most suitable word from the vocab list in the spaces below. You might need to change the form of the word; for instance, walk might become walked.

1. Vanessa walked ……………………..……. to the station as she was determined not to miss the next train.

2. I knew I should ……………………………….. to having thrown an egg at the neighbour's window.

3. The art teacher encouraged the students to draw using sticks of …………...…………… as it was effective for shading and blending.

4. Simon left the party early so that the loud music did not ……………………..… his headache.

5. Danny was completely ………………………...…….. by the difficult clues in the crossword puzzle.

6. The powerful ……………………..……. of pine trees fills the air in the forest.

7. The poem is full of ……………………..……. phrases describing the beauty of nature.

8. The ……………………………. old car which my grandfather had owned for twenty years finally refused to start.

9. The Blair family have lived in the same village for several ……………………………s.

10. The dancer spent hours practising in order to …………………………..………… and perfect his movements.

Exercise C

Select the most suitable word from the choice provided.

1. There was an unpleasant ……………………………...… coming from the drains.

    a: odour   **b: eloquent**   **c: briskly**

2. The role of an editor is to help authors ……………………………...……… their work ready for publication.

    a: refine   **b: decrepit**   **c: generation**

3. Several ………...……………….s of the elephant herd have lived in the national park.

    a: generation   **b: briskly**   **c: refine**

4. The recipe for meringues said to beat the egg whites ……………………...………….. until they formed soft peaks.

    a: briskly   **b: aggravate**   **c: eloquent**

5. The restaurant installed a special grill which burned ………………..………….. to give a smoky flavour to their steaks.

    a: charcoal   **b: decrepit**   **c: refine**

6. The criminal decided to …………………...…………. to his crime as he hoped his jail sentence would be shorter.

    a: confess   **b: odour**   **c: generation**

7. Freya gave me an …………………………………. description of her delicious five-course lunch.

    a: confess   **b: refine**   **c: eloquent**

8. The Poulter family bought a ………………...……….. house and then spent a year renovating it before moving in.

    a: generation   **b: charcoal**   **c: decrepit**

9. The child looked totally ………………...………..…… as she clearly did not understand a word that the French teacher was saying.

    a: bewildered   **b: confess**   **c: refine**

10. Emily's brother knew how to ………………..……….. her with his cheeky comments.

    a: decrepit   **b: odour**   **c aggravate**

Vocab 11

Notes

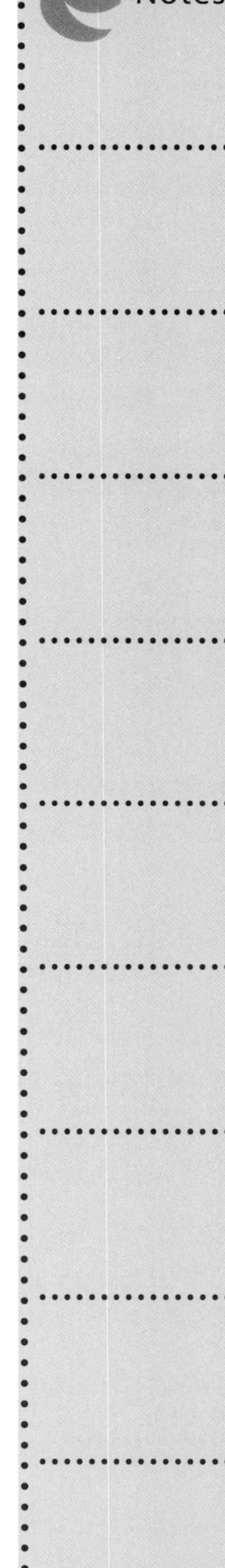

35

Vocabulary 12

Learn the following words and then answer the questions.

1. **Eminent** (adj.): very important, famous, illustrious, prominent.

   The town hall contains statues of many <u>eminent</u> men and women who contributed to the history of the area.

2. **Bacteria** (plural) (n.): microbes, germs, types of organism. (singular: bacterium)

   Duncan works in a lab where he studies infectious diseases caused by viruses and <u>bacteria</u>.

3. **Eliminate** (v.): remove, eradicate, defeat, kill.

   Hounslow Academy managed to <u>eliminate</u> their opponents from the London schools' football championships.

4. **Seclusion** (n.): privacy, isolation, shelter.

   My grandparents liked to holiday in <u>seclusion</u> in their log cabin near the summit of a mountain.

5. **Vulture** (n.): large bird of prey (raptor) feeding mainly from carcasses, a scavenger, an unpleasant person who exploits others.

   In Nature, <u>vultures</u> serve a useful function because they clean up the remains of dead animals.

6. **Belittle** (v.): undermine, bully, put down, minimise someone's achievements or character.

   Jack tried to <u>belittle</u> his sister's amazing grades at school out of jealousy.

7. **Integrity** (n.): honesty, honour, principle, virtue.

   Isla is a woman of <u>integrity</u>, because she is honest and reliable.

8. **Autopsy** (n.): the examination of a dead body by dissection to discover the cause of death, post-mortem, analysis.

   The <u>autopsy</u> proved that Joe's murderer had struck him on the head with an iron bar.

9. **Accession** (n.): time when a position of power or rank begins, formal acceptance of an agreement, inauguration.

   We celebrated the 50th anniversary of the Queen's <u>accession</u> to the throne in 2002.

10. **Earshot** (n.): range within which a voice can be heard, hearing, range.

    When she came within <u>earshot</u> of the group, Tina heard her name mentioned.

Notes

Synonym Exercise A

Write the word from the vocab list which is most **similar** in meaning next to each word listed below.

1. Undermine...
2. Isolation ....
3. Eradicate ....
4. Post-mortem ....
5. Germs ....
6. Honour ....
7. Inauguration ....
8. Prominent ....
9. Overhearing ....
10. Scavenger ....

Exercise B

Write the most suitable word from the vocab list in the spaces below. You might need to change the form of the word; for instance, walk might become walked.

1. Dad said his unpleasant boss always found a member of staff to ……………………….. and bully.

2. Albert Einstein was one of the most ………………………………….. physicists of the twentieth century, and won the Nobel Prize in 1921.

3. The teachers' loud quarrel distracted every student within ……………………………….

4. Chloe acted with ………………………………….. and admitted that she ought to be punished for the offence instead of her friend.

5. The detectives were shocked when the ………………………………… showed that the cause of death was poison.

6. Some ……………………………….. have developed into untreatable superbugs because of our overuse of antibiotics.

7. The secret agent managed to complete the mission and ………………………………. her target without being spotted by security.

8. The ……………………………….s circled above the carcasses of the dead zebras.

9. In January 2016, Spain and Portugal celebrated the thirty-year anniversary of their …………………….………. to the EU.

10. The monks live in complete ……………………………..... for the duration of their training, in order to pray and study in peace.

Vocab 12

Cut-and-keep

- eminent
- bacteria
- eliminate
- seclusion
- vulture
- belittle
- integrity
- autopsy
- accession
- earshot

Exercise C

Select the most suitable word from the choice provided.

1. Raw chicken contains harmful …………..…………..….. called salmonella.
   - a: bacteria
   - b: belittle
   - c: accession

2. ………………………..…s rarely attack healthy animals; instead they hunt the wounded or sick.
   - a: seclusion
   - b: vulture
   - c: bacteria

3. Today's lecture on the French Revolution will be given by the …………..………..… historian Simon Schama.
   - a: eminent
   - b: belittle
   - c: vulture

4. The …………….………… revealed that Millie's grandmother had died of natural causes.
   - a: accession
   - b: seclusion
   - c: autopsy

5. Sometimes Abdul missed the ……………..…………… of the countryside where he had grown up, compared to the busy streets of London where he now lived.
   - a: seclusion
   - b: accession
   - c: integrity

6. Mr Parker was an excellent teacher: he would always encourage us and never ……………...…………….. our achievements.
   - a: belittle
   - b: vulture
   - c: seclusion

7. My mother told me to always act with ………………..…..…… and stay true to myself.
   - a: eliminate
   - b: belittle
   - c: integrity

8. The girls made sure they were not within ………………..………….. of their friend as they made plans for her surprise birthday party.
   - a: earshot
   - b: integrity
   - c: eliminate

9. The police could safely ………………………..……… the person they arrested as a suspect after discovering he had an alibi at the time of the robbery.
   - a: belittle
   - b: eliminate
   - c: accession

10. Elizabeth I's …………………..…….. to the throne in 1558 marked the start of a Golden Age for England.
    - a: eminent
    - b: accession
    - c: seclusion

Vocabulary 13

Learn the following words and then answer the questions.

1. **Pertinent** (adj.): relevant, suitable, applicable.

   The detective ensured the quick success of the investigation by focusing on the pertinent facts of the case.

2. **Ravine** (n.): a deep gorge often created by a stream or river, abyss, chasm.

   We threw stones down into the ravine while standing on the cliff edge.

3. **Gastric** (adj.): relating to the stomach, abdominal.

   John had stomach problems for years before a gastric specialist made an accurate diagnosis.

4. **Resourceful** (adj.): imaginative, active, creative, inventive.

   The hikers needed to be resourceful in order to survive, after a landslide trapped them in a cave.

5. **Eavesdrop** (v.): to listen without permission, overhear, snoop.

   Jenny used to sneakily eavesdrop outside the door when her brother's friends were in his bedroom.

6. **Carnage** (n.): the killing of a large number of people, massacre, destruction, havoc, slaughter.

   There was carnage near the coral reef as two great white sharks began to attack each other.

7. **Anarchy** (n.): absence of government, lawlessness, rebellion, revolution.

   After the president was assassinated, the country fell into a state of anarchy as no alternative leader came forward.

8. **Affiliate** (v.): to associate with, connect, partner, collaborate.

   My sister's charity group is completely independent and does not affiliate itself with any political party.

9. **Pictorial** (adj.): expressed in pictures, graphic, illustrative.

   My great-grandfather was a keen photographer so there is a fantastic pictorial record of our family history.

10. **Accentuate** (v.): focus attention on, emphasise, highlight, make clear.

    The politician accentuated the government's achievements whilst ignoring the well-known problems.

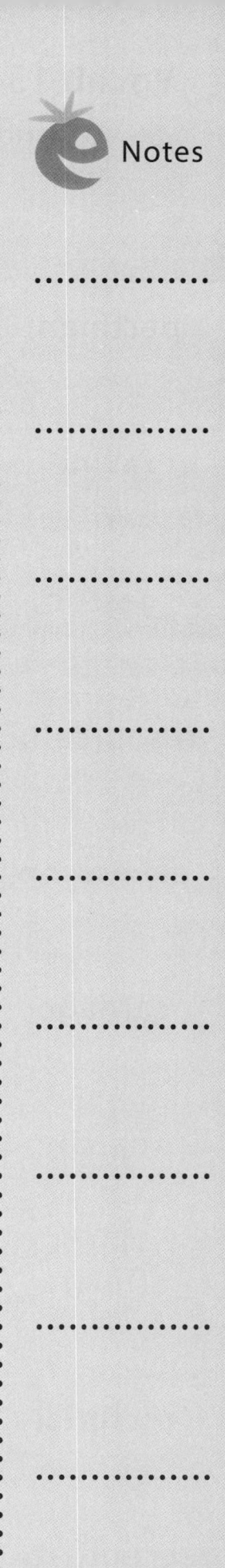

Notes

Vocab 13
Cut-and-keep

- pertinent
- ravine
- gastric
- resourceful
- eavesdrop
- carnage
- anarchy
- affiliate
- pictorial
- accentuate

Synonym Exercise A

Write the word from the vocab list which is most **similar** in meaning next to each word listed below.

1. Highlight ....
2. Relevant ....
3. Lawlessness ....
4. Gorge ....
5. Illustrative ....
6. Inventive ....
7. Overhear ....
8. Collaborate ....
9. Slaughter ....
10. Abdominal ....

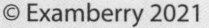

Exercise B

Write the most suitable word from the vocab list in the spaces below. You might need to change the form of the word; for instance, walk might become walked.

1. The driver lost control on the winding road and the car skidded off the cliff and into the ……………………………

2. Emma taught her children to be ……………………………….. , and so they learned to find imaginative ways of solving problems.

3. The police thought Dominic was involved in the robbery as he had previously been ……………………………..d with the gang leader.

4. Mum complained that the unflattering photo I took seemed to ………………….………….. her double chin!

5. Zoe pressed her ear to keyhole in order to ……………………………. on her parents' conversation about her school report.

6. The politician only answered the ………………………………. questions on her homelessness policy, and ignored spurious remarks about her appearance.

7. The ……………………...…………… novel was a hit with those who preferred stories told in images.

8. Jessie had ……………………..………. flu, which caused stomach pains and vomiting.

9. The war was over, and finally the …………………………… on the battlefields ceased.

10. The reign of King Stephen I in England was known for its lawlessness and ……………………………….

Exercise C

Select the most suitable word from the choice provided.

1. The Red Cross stated that it would take months to clean up the .... caused by the earthquake.

    a: ravine **b: carnage** **c: gastric**

2. The scholarship candidate was a bright student and asked many .... questions.

    a: eavesdrop **b: affiliate** **c: pertinent**

3. My tummy wouldn't stop rumbling so I had to have a check-up with the doctor of .... medicine.

    a: gastric **b: pertinent** **c: affiliate**

4. There was complete .... in the classroom when the usual teacher was away.

    a: eavesdrop **b: pertinent** **c: anarchy**

5. The local football club was independent and did not .... itself with any particular school in the area.

    a: affiliate **b: resourceful** **c: ravine**

6. Whilst marooned on a desert island, the Robinson Family was very .... and built an amazing treehouse out of driftwood.

    a: resourceful **b: anarchy** **c: pertinent**

7. The problem with having such thin walls is that it is very easy for people to .... on our conversations.

    a: eavesdrop **b: ravine** **c: pictorial**

8. Bertie's bright red trousers seemed to .... his long, skinny legs.

    a: affiliate **b: accentuate** **c: anarchy**

9. Pablo decided to walk down through the rocky .... and then stop for a picnic near the waterfall.

    a: ravine **b: pertinent** **c: gastric**

10. Cave paintings give a .... representation of the lives of Stone Age people.

    a: carnage **b: pictorial** **c: affiliate**

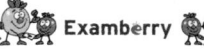

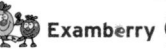

Vocab 13

Notes

Vocabulary 14

Learn the following words and then answer the questions.

1. **Orator** (n.): a person who is skilled at public speaking, an eloquent speaker.

   The successful orator inspired the whole audience with her impressive speech.

2. **Loot** (v.): rob, plunder, raid.

   During the riot, many people began to loot and steal from the abandoned shops.

3. **Onus** (n.): a burden, responsibility, obligation.

   The onus is on the pharmacist to ensure the correct medication is given to customers.

4. **Conserve** (v.): save, protect, sustain, preserve.

   Governments must do all they can to help conserve rainforests and slow down global warming.

5. **Affectionate** (adj.): caring, friendly, loving.

   Jenny was very affectionate towards her pet dog and always let her sleep on the bed.

6. **Exuberant** (adj.): full of energy, excited, enthusiastic, buoyant.

   Anna was exuberant and joyful when she heard that her parents were taking her to Barbados on holiday.

7. **Amnesia** (n.): partial or total loss of memory, forgetfulness, blankness.

   James had amnesia after the car accident; he couldn't remember how it had happened.

8. **Truncate** (v.): shorten, abbreviate, curtail.

   I had to truncate my article because it was too long for publication.

9. **Thwart** (v.): prevent, hinder, defeat.

   The evil villain's plan was thwarted because the heroine was one step ahead of him.

10. **Bombard** (v.): attack continuously, address continuously, blitz.

    The media bombards people with Christmas advertisements from September until Christmas Eve!

Synonym Exercise A

Write the word from the vocab list which is most **similar** in meaning next to each word listed below.

1. Burden..
2. Blitz..
3. Speaker ....
4. Excited..
5. Abbreviate..
6. Plunder...
7. Loving...
8. Hinder...
9. Save..
10. Forgetfulness...

Exercise B

Write the most suitable word from the vocab list in the spaces below. You might need to change the form of the word; for instance, walk might become walked.

1. The .... puppy would not stop licking my face and nuzzling me.
2. Sandra was clearly the best .... and deserved to win the school debate.
3. The bank robbers were ....ed by the employee who set off the alarm system.
4. The invaders arrived to .... the golden palace, immediately smashing their way in to find the famous statues.
5. The film director was forced to .... the movie because audiences simply found it too long.
6. The travel writer was .... in her praise of the luxurious cruise ship.
7. It is important to remember that the .... is on students to revise before the final exams.
8. After the plane crash, the confused pilot was found wandering across the moors, lost and suffering from ....
9. The reporters will .... the actor with questions about the recent scandal as soon as he leaves home.
10. Mo needed to rest and .... his energy before the half-marathon.

Vocab 14

Cut-and-keep

- orator
- loot
- onus
- conserve
- affectionate
- exuberant
- amnesia
- truncate
- thwart
- bombard

© Examberry 2021

Vocab 14

Exercise C

Select the most suitable word from the choice provided.

1. Lucy was a bright student but she had a tendency to ………………………… the teacher with irrelevant questions.

    a: conserve   b: bombard   c: exuberant

2. During the drought in July, the government advised people to ………………..…….. water by taking showers instead of baths.

    a: onus   b: loot   c: conserve

3. The Viking warriors arrived at night to ………………...………. the village and burn the crops.

    a: amnesia   b: affectionate   c: loot

4. In order to ……………...……………………… the enemy troops, the captain ordered his men to destroy the bridge behind them.

    a: thwart   b: loot   c: bombard

5. Jimmy was very ………………...…………… towards his little sister and gave her lots of cuddles.

    a: conserve   b: affectionate   c: onus

6. Winston Churchill was known to be a great ………………………………….. and to inspire the public with his speeches.

    a: orator   b: thwart   c: exuberant

7. Mrs Devlin is the Headmistress, so the …………………………….….. is on her to make all important decisions regarding the school.

    a: onus   b: loot   c: affectionate

8. Billy experienced partial …………………………… after falling off a ladder and hitting his head.

    a: conserve   b: exuberant   c: amnesia

9. The summer cricket tour was ………………...…………d by a series of violent storms.

    a: amnesia   b: truncate   c: loot

10. Lara's …………………….… dancing and perfect technique meant that she won the ballet prize.

    a: conserve   b: exuberant   c: onus

Vocabulary 15

Learn the following words and then answer the questions.

1. **Ligament** (n.): a short band of strong tissue which connects two bones or holds together a joint, sinew.

   Tom, the star striker, tore a <u>ligament</u> in a football match and was out of action for six months.

2. **Endowment** (n.): income or property that is given to someone, inheritance, grant, gift.

   The billionaire set up an <u>endowment</u> which supported his old school.

3. **Ruthless** (adj.): brutal, merciless, cut-throat, unforgiving.

   The evil king was <u>ruthless</u> when punishing his enemies; all of whom were imprisoned for life.

4. **Detriment** (n.): disadvantage, impairment, damage.

   The doctor advised the patient that drinking tea was harmless and did not pose a <u>detriment</u> to his health.

5. **Haggard** (adj.): worn and gaunt in appearance, exhausted, weakened.

   The make-up artist transformed the young actor into a <u>haggard</u> old woman.

6. **Propensity** (n.): an inclination to behave in a certain way, tendency.

   Andrew had a <u>propensity</u> to blush whenever he felt shy or embarrassed.

7. **Coalition** (n.): alliance, union, partnership.

   After the general election no political party had an overall majority and so a <u>coalition</u> was formed.

8. **Dissect** (v.): to take apart or to pieces, to dismember; analyse in detail.

   We had to <u>dissect</u> a frog in our biology class to view the contents of its stomach.

9. **Maul** (v.): to inflict a wound; to treat something roughly.

   I watched the dog <u>maul</u> the chew toy and fling it across the room.

10. **Epitome** (n.): a person or thing that is a perfect example of a particular quality, essence.

    The princess was the <u>epitome</u> of elegance in her stunning wedding dress.

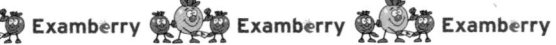

Notes

Vocab 15
Cut-and-keep

ligament

ruthless

endowment

detriment

haggard

propensity

coalition

dissect

maul

epitome

Synonym Exercise A

Write the word from the vocab list which is most **similar** in meaning next to each word listed below.

1. Disadvantage ....
2. Tendency ....
3. Merciless ....
4. Injure ....
5. Union ....
6. Gaunt ....
7. Essence ....
8. Gift ....
9. Analyse ....
10. Connective tissue ....

Exercise B

Write the most suitable word from the vocab list in the spaces below. You might need to change the form of the word; for instance, walk might become walked.

1. Julian had a ……………………………. to overreact and lost his temper when anyone criticised him.

2. A female bear may ……………………………… anyone who approaches when she is protecting her cubs.

3. The …………………………….. rebel leader ordered the expulsion of the entire royal family from the country.

4. Even under great pressure, the emergency doctor was the ………………………………. of professionalism.

5. The university …………………………….. was provided by a wealthy family to support students in financial need.

6. As you get older your muscles and ……………………………….s become weaker.

7. Joshua's obsession with computer games takes up all his time, much to the ………………………….. of his schoolwork.

8. In English today, we ………………….....…….ed the poem in great detail in order to fully appreciate and understand it.

9. The pupils looked ……………………………... and exhausted after their final exam.

10. Mr Sandhu led a ……………………………. of school head teachers, working to share playing fields and other resources.

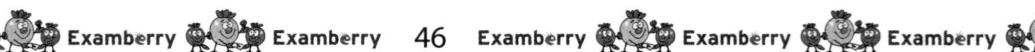

Exercise C

Select the most suitable word from the choice provided.

1. The botanist began to .... the plant under a microscope, in order to examine its delicate parts.

    a: ruthless   **b: dissect**   **c: detriment**

2. Tom returned to his family looking rather .... after a year backpacking abroad.

    a: dissect   **b: endowment**   **c: haggard**

3. The film has had rave reviews and is the .... of a classic romantic drama.

    a: endowment   **b: ligament**   **c: epitome**

4. A .... of environmental groups is working on plans to reduce river pollution.

    a: haggard   **b: dissect**   **c: coalition**

5. Jackson's .... to lie is going to get him into trouble one day.

    a: maul   **b: detriment**   **c: propensity**

6. It is common for athletes to damage their ....s at some stage in their career due to their intense training programmes.

    a: epitome   **b: ligament**   **c: dissect**

7. A child fell into the lion's enclosure, but luckily a security guard rescued him from being ....ed by the animals.

    a: maul   **b: ligament**   **c: endowment**

8. Before we moved to Spain, Mum was .... about throwing out old clothes and toys, so that we only took essential items with us.

    a: ligament   **b: ruthless**   **c: maul**

9. The successful musician set up an .... to support the school's music centre.

    a: endowment   **b: detriment**   **c: dissect**

10. The factory used toxic chemicals, much to the .... of the local air quality.

    a: detriment   **b: haggard**   **c: propensity**

Vocab 15

Notes

Vocabulary 16

Learn the following words and then answer the questions.

1. **Denote** (v.): stand for, indicate, signify, symbolise.

   When the pirates buried the treasure, they marked an X on the map to denote its location.

2. **Equity** (n.): fair justice; the value of shares issued by a company, value of property.

   A basic principle at our school is the equity of treatment that all pupils receive.

3. **Dissertation** (n.): extended essay, thesis.

   Many students of English have written a dissertation on the works of William Shakespeare.

4. **Adamant** (adj.): refusing to be persuaded or to change one's mind, resolute, determined, insistent.

   The local residents were adamant that they would not allow the council to knock down the town library.

5. **Parachute** (v.): drop from an aircraft by parachute, be appointed or appoint someone in an emergency situation.

   The pilot was forced to parachute from his aircraft after its propeller was destroyed by enemy gunfire.

6. **Monetary** (adj.): relating to or involving money, financial.

   The government's monetary policy was a disaster, as they had borrowed far too much money and the country was in great debt.

7. **Combustion** (n.): the process of burning, ignition, fire.

   We know now that the combustion of fossil fuels causes harmful emissions which contribute to global warming.

8. **Delinquent** (adj.): irresponsible, criminal, lawbreaking.

   The delinquent young man is being monitored by police after he smashed windows and caused a fight in the town centre.

9. **Defensible** (adj.): justifiable by argument, plausible; secure, fortified.

   After Dora admitted to starting the fire, the Headmaster's decision to expel her seemed reasonable and defensible.

10. **Extension** (n.): continuation, expansion, increase, addition.

    Martha requested an extension of two days to complete her homework because she had been unwell.

Synonym Exercise A

Write the word from the vocab list which is most **similar** in meaning next to each word listed below.

1. Essay ....
2. Criminal..
3. Signify..
4. Fairness ....
5. Increase..
6. Justifiable ....
7. Determined ....
8. Burning ....
9. Financial...
10. Drop ....

Exercise B

Write the most suitable word from the vocab list in the spaces below. You might need to change the form of the word; for instance, walk might become walked.

1. Victorian literature includes many examples of spontaneous ...., meaning that characters explode into flames for no apparent reason.

2. The sixth-formers were required to write a ……………………………….. of 5,000 words on their chosen subject.

3. The Prime Minister is ……………………………. that she will not resign, despite her unpopularity.

4. House-owners must obtain planning permission in order to build an ………………….. to their property.

5. The play was about a ……………………..………. young girl who had been pressured into a life of crime by evil gang members.

6. Aisha's silver ring had sentimental value but very little ………………………………. worth.

7. A castle built on an island is easily ………………………………. .

8. Planes were sent to ……………….……...…………. in first-aid supplies to the war-torn region.

9. Dan had paid off the loan on his house and so had acquired a large amount of
…………….………...……. .

10. The hoisting of the Royal Standard flag over Buckingham Palace ………………………..s that the Queen is in residence.

Vocab 16

Cut-and-keep

denote

equity

dissertation

adamant

parachute

monetary

combustion

delinquent

defensible

extension

Vocab 16

Exercise C

Select the most suitable word from the choice provided.

1. Flynn's ambition was to one day ………………………………. out of a plane.

    a: dissertation   b: parachute   c: defensible

2. Before a common currency was established in Britain, different areas used their own ………………………………. systems.

    a: equity   b: combustion   c: monetary

3. In a ……………………..……….. reaction, substances react with oxygen and generate light and heat.

    a: extension   b: combustion   c: delinquent

4. Joanne was a history student and decided to write her ……………………...…………. on a topic relating to the First World War.

    a: dissertation   b: defensible   c: extension

5. Anti-Discrimination laws in the workplace are designed to ensure employees are treated with ………………………...……., regardless of race, age or gender.

    a: denote   b: equity   c: extension

6. During the January Sales, red labels on clothing ……………………………………. that these items have been reduced by 50%.

    a: denote   b: combustion   c: monetary

7. London Underground announced that an ……………………………. would be built to the Jubilee Line.

    a: extension   b: dissertation   c: delinquent

8. Victoria had broken her arm twice playing rugby, but she was ………………...………… that she would never give up the sport.

    a: monetary   b: parachute   c: adamant

9. John was the mentor in charge of rehabilitation for …………………………………….. teenagers.

    a: delinquent   b: extension   c: adamant

10. Slavery is not and has never been morally …………………………………. .

    a: combustion   b: monetary   c: defensible

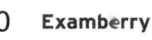

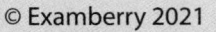

Vocabulary 17

Learn the following words and then answer the questions.

1. **Outcry** (n.): uproar, protest, objection.

   The bombing caused an international <u>outcry</u> because innocent citizens were killed.

2. **Admirable** (adj.): deserving respect or approval, worthy, commendable, honourable.

   Jackie made the <u>admirable</u> decision to donate her birthday money to Cancer Research, instead of buying something for herself.

3. **Casket** (n.): a small box for holding valuables, case, chest.

   Many ancient cultures made jewelled <u>caskets</u> for their most precious belongings.

4. **Perpetual** (adj.): never-ending or changing, continuous, everlasting.

   The White Queen's harsh rule manifested itself across the land of Narnia as <u>perpetual</u> winter.

5. **Dire** (adj.): extremely serious or urgent; of very poor quality.

   The starving family were in <u>dire</u> need of help from the foodbank.

6. **Abrasive** (adj.): harsh, rough, sharp, scratchy.

   Sally had a rather <u>abrasive</u> personality; she often upset people unintentionally.

7. **Archaeology** (n.): The physical study of history and prehistory through excavation of sites.

   After visiting the restored remains of a Roman villa, my cousin became fascinated by ancient history and <u>archaeology</u>.

8. **Barometer** (n.): An instrument for measuring atmospheric pressure, to predict the weather, or something which reflects changes in taste or opinion.

   Just as the <u>barometer</u> had indicated, the storm rolled in quickly.

9. **Prudent** (adj.): acting with caution, sensible, wise.

   Jane was usually <u>prudent</u> with her pocket money, but could not resist the expensive purple sequinned pencil case.

10. **Storey** (n.): floor, level, tier.

    A new twenty-<u>storey</u> apartment building loomed over the historic Victorian town centre.

Vocab 17
Cut-and-keep

- outcry
- admirable
- casket
- perpetual
- dire
- abrasive
- archaeology
- barometer
- prudent
- storey

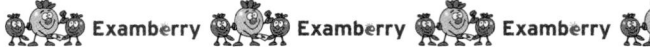

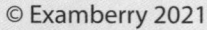

Synonym Exercise A

Write the word from the vocab list which is most **similar** in meaning next to each word listed below.

1. Serious ....
2. Harsh ....
3. Wise ....
4. Never-ending ....
5. Level ....
6. Protest ....
7. Box ....
8. Honourable ....
9. Instrument ....
10. Excavation ....

Exercise B

Write the most suitable word from the vocab list in the spaces below. You might need to change the form of the word; for instance, walk might become walked.

1. The new multi-........................ car park next to the shopping centre is a monstrosity and blocks the beautiful view of the lake.

2. A public .... by the shop's customers forced the owners to lower their prices.

3. Some people say that .... is the purest form of history as you can touch artefacts from the past.

4. The explorers found an ancient wooden .... containing three perfect sapphires in the cave.

5. It is .... to keep your bags with you at all times when in busy locations so as to deter pickpockets.

6. Alice's determination and courage in the face of disaster was ....

7. In politics, the .... of public opinion rarely remains stable for long but swings between parties and politicians at a moment's notice.

8. The government promised that anyone caught breaking the new law would face .... consequences.

9. The country seems to be in a state of .... war and chaos, with no sign of peace in sight.

10. The carpenter smoothed the wood with fine yet .... sandpaper.

Exercise C

Select the most suitable word from the choice provided.

1. The family lived on the third floor of a five-………………….. house that had been converted into flats.

    a: storey **b: prudent** **c: outcry**

2. Charlotte's grandfather liked to be prepared for all kinds of weather and so kept a …………………….…….. hanging in his front hall.

    a: admirable **b: barometer** **c: outcry**

3. You should only call an ambulance in ………..………….. emergencies and not when you have stubbed your toe!

    a: outcry **b: archaeology** **c: dire**

4. Thanks to its brilliant department of …………………………....….., the museum has a new section displaying Egyptian mummies.

    a: archaeology **b: dire** **c: barometer**

5. Jeffrey was a grumpy looking man: he had hard, cold eyes and his mouth was set in a ……………………….. sneer.

    a: perpetual **b: prudent** **c: storey**

6. In The Merchant of Venice, Portia's suitors are made to choose between a …………………………. of gold, silver or lead before being permitted to marry her.

    a: casket **b: archaeology** **c: outcry**

7. My boss has an ………………..…………. attitude and is always shouting at me for the smallest mistakes.

    a: dire **b: abrasive** **c: barometer**

8. John's refusal to take the easy option and work for his family's company is ……………………….. ; it is clear that he wants to make his own way in the world.

    a: admirable **b: archaeology** **c: prudent**

9. The Enclosures Act of the eighteenth century caused a public…………………….., because it removed the right of ordinary people to graze their animals on common land.

    a: outcry **b: prudent** **c: perpetual**

10. Kevin was a ……………………….. solo traveller and took care to avoid potentially dangerous situations.

    a: admirable **b: casket** **c: prudent**

Vocab 17

Notes

Vocabulary 18

Learn the following words and then answer the questions.

1. **Platonic** (adj.): affectionate but not romantic, friendly.

    My sister developed great <u>platonic</u> friendships with her university flatmates; they all came to her wedding.

2. **Denounce** (v.): to point out or publicly declare to be wrong or evil, inform against, condemn.

    The dictator made a speech to <u>denounce</u> the actions of his enemies.

3. **Blasé** (adj.): indifferent to, casual, unconcerned.

    After a few years the actor became used to being followed around by paparazzi; he is now very <u>blasé</u> about having his photo taken.

4. **Throttle** (v.): strangle, choke, smother.

    The defendant admitted that he had tried to <u>throttle</u> the burglar but declared that he had only done so in self-defence.

5. **Intestine** (v.): tubes in the body through which food passes when it has left the stomach, internal organs, guts.

    The tapeworm was an inhabitant of the dog's <u>intestine</u>.

6. **Outermost** (adj.): the one that is furthest from the centre.

    We know very little about the <u>outermost</u> regions of the universe.

7. **Aggrieved** (adj.): hurt, upset, pained, resentful.

    Even though they had been distant for years, Zoe was <u>aggrieved</u> that she had not been invited to her sister's wedding.

8. **Grandeur** (n.): splendour, magnificence, opulence.

    The majestic <u>grandeur</u> of the Roman villa was a sight I would never forget.

9. **Ethical** (adj.): moral, good; relating to moral principles.

    Some people don't eat meat because of their <u>ethical</u> beliefs that animals shouldn't be killed.

10. **Equitable** (adj.): fair, just, proper, honest.

    Society is increasingly <u>equitable</u> for people of different races and genders.

Vocab 18

Cut-and-keep

platonic

denounce

blasé

throttle

intestine

outermost

aggrieved

grandeur

ethical

equitable

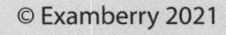

Synonym Exercise A

Write the word from the vocab list which is most **similar** in meaning next to each word listed below.

1. Strangle ....
2. Furthest ....
3. Casual ....
4. Guts ....
5. Friendly ....
6. Splendour ....
7. Just ....
8. Moral ....
9. Pained ....
10. Condemn ....

Exercise B

Write the most suitable word from the vocab list in the spaces below. You might need to change the form of the word; for instance, walk might become walked.

1. Freddie's tie got caught around his neck and he felt as though he was being ....d.

2. Priests took the risk and ....d their bishop to the King for the crime of heresy.

3. The victim's family became .... when the judge did not give the assailant a harsher sentence.

4. I only managed to hit the .... ring of the archery target on my first try.

5. Noah was so .... about the world of work that he expected a job to simply land in his lap!

6. The minister's effort to create an .... justice system was hampered by systematic corruption.

7. It is not .... to promote harmful substances so advertisements for cigarettes are illegal.

8. The hotel, which had once been the home of royalty, had an air of faded ....

9. Although the couple divorced, they maintain a .... relationship.

10. Food passes from the stomach to the small .... where ninety percent of it is digested.

Vocab 18

Exercise C

Select the most suitable word from the choice provided.

1. Everyone thought that Jack and Jill were a couple but their relationship was purely ……………………………. .

    a: throttle   **b: grandeur**   **c: platonic**

2. Despite winning the popular vote, the Conservatives ……………………………..d their former leader.

    a: blasé   **b: aggrieved**   **c: denounce**

3. Mary's ……………………………. attitude when ordering the most expensive dish on the menu angered Jonathan, who was paying.

    a: ethical   **b: intestine**   **c: blasé**

4. The question of whether or not to test new medicine on animals is a controversial ………………..……. debate.

    a: ethical   **b: grandeur**   **c: equitable**

5. Before the French Revolution, King Louis XVI and Marie Antoinette lived in luxury and ………..…………………. in the Palace of Versailles.

    a: blasé   **b: ethical**   **c: grandeur**

6. The villagers felt ……………………….. at the council's decision to build a new block of flats by the river, which would spoil the landscape.

    a: grandeur   **b: aggrieved**   **c: outermost**

7. When the small ……………………..….is stretched out it, it is about 22 feet long!

    a: intestine   **b: platonic**   **c: ethical**

8. Jess likes her new colleague, although his constant complaining occasionally makes her want to ………..………..……. him!

    a: throttle   **b: intestine**   **c: equitable**

9. Exfoliating scrubs can be used to get rid of the dry…………..………….. layer of skin, but it is important to moisturise afterwards.

    a: outermost   **b: throttle**   **c: grandeur**

10. The purpose of the conference was to discuss plans for a more …………..…………. distribution of wealth and power among nations.

    a: ethical   **b: equitable**   **c: outermost**

Vocabulary 19

Learn the following words and then answer the questions.

1. **Infest** (v.): to be present in large numbers, usually causing a problem or damage, overrun.

   At least four species of fleas which <u>infest</u> the common rat are known to bite humans.

2. **Frankness** (n.): the quality of being open, honest and direct.

   Michael spoke to the group about his fears with a <u>frankness</u> that was refreshing to witness.

3. **Curator** (n.): person in charge of a collection in a museum or library, guardian, director.

   The <u>curator</u> of the National Portrait Gallery is responsible for some priceless paintings.

4. **Astound** (v.): amaze, shock, bewilder, confuse.

   The magician's illusion <u>astounded</u> the crowd; people were unable to imagine how she had escaped.

5. **Strenuous** (adj.): requiring or using great effort, taxing, demanding, exhausting.

   The doctor advised Catherine to avoid any <u>strenuous</u> exercise for the next month while her sprained ankle healed.

6. **Relinquish** (v.): to give up, abandon, renounce.

   No matter how hard it may seem, don't <u>relinquish</u> your dream of becoming a vet.

7. **Culminate** (v.): to come together, come to a climax, end up, finish.

   At the end of the night, the concert will <u>culminate</u> in a huge fireworks display.

8. **Fathom** (v.): understand, grasp, comprehend.

   For years people have been trying to <u>fathom</u> the mysteries of the deep ocean.

9. **Antiseptic** (adj.): kills harmful germs, disinfectant, sterile, clean.

   The treatment consists of removing the cause of the infection and cleaning the skin with <u>antiseptic</u> wipes.

10. **Rummage** (v.): to search untidily through something, delve, hunt through.

    My granny asked me to open the chest and <u>rummage</u> around to find her magnifying glass.

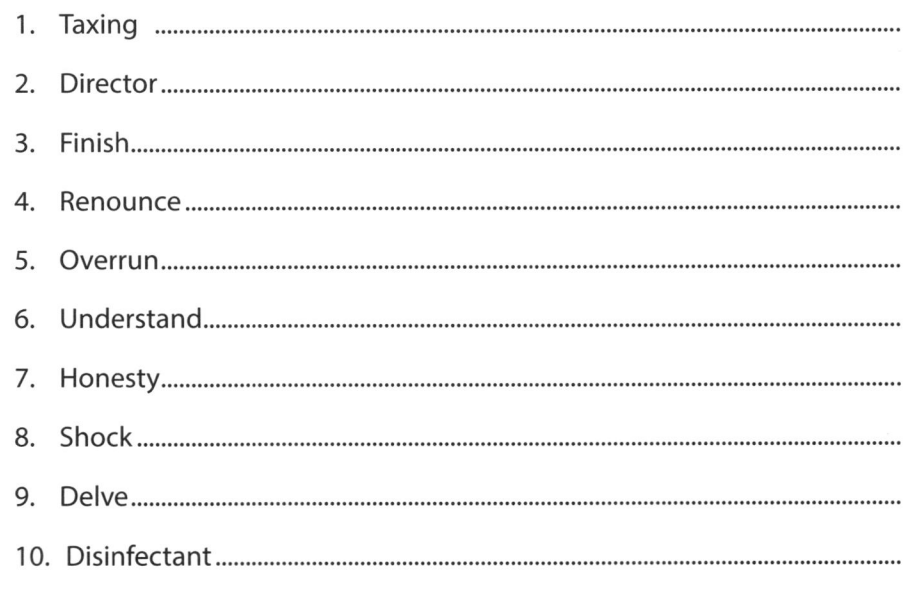

Vocab 19

Cut-and-keep

- infest
- frankness
- curator
- astound
- strenuous
- relinquish
- culminate
- fathom
- antiseptic
- rummage

Synonym Exercise A

Write the word from the vocab list which is most **similar** in meaning next to each word listed below.

1. Taxing ....
2. Director ....
3. Finish ....
4. Renounce ....
5. Overrun ....
6. Understand ....
7. Honesty ....
8. Shock ....
9. Delve ....
10. Disinfectant ....

Exercise B

Write the most suitable word from the vocab list in the spaces below. You might need to change the form of the word; for instance, walk might become walked.

1. Savlon is a popular ……………………….…. cream used to sterilise cuts.
2. The successful car salesman was known for his …………………………….. about the condition of the used vehicles in his showroom.
3. In many cities, cockroaches ………………………………. entire buildings.
4. In order to join the military you have to be prepared to undergo ……………………… exercise.
5. The price tag on the designer dress will ………..………………. most followers of fashion.
6. I have always worked diligently and therefore cannot ……………………………… why my boss just fired me.
7. Following the Hundred Years' War, England was forced to ………………………………. its claims to the Duchy of Normandy in France.
8. Foxes often ………………………………. through rubbish bins at night-time to find food.
9. All Jane's efforts during the trial ……………………….d in success and led to her promotion.
10. The ………………………. proudly guided us round the gallery, showing off the most famous paintings in the impressive collection.

Exercise C

Select the most suitable word from the choice provided.

1. Emma appreciated colleagues who spoke with ………………………. about their work progress, rather than skirting around the truth.

    a: frankness   **b: strenuous**   **c: relinquish**

2. Many dictators are so determined not to ………………………….. power that they imprison their enemies and repress free speech.

    a: rummage   **b: relinquish**   **c: curator**

3. Walter hoped that all his studying would ………………….....……. in an impressive exam performance.

    a: culminate   **b: infest**   **c: frankness**

4. ……………..……………….. wipes are convenient for cleaning kitchens but are bad for the environment.

    a: culminate   **b: fathom**   **c: antiseptic**

5. Pia forgot to wear her Halloween costume to school but was told to have a ………………….....…….. in the dressing-up box and choose what she wanted.

    a: rummage   **b: frankness**   **c: antiseptic**

6. Dad said the most ……………………… thing he had done all day was mow the lawn.

    a: strenuous   **b: culminate**   **c: frankness**

7. It is hard to …………………………….. Jai's motives for shoplifting: he has plenty of money and no previous criminal convictions.

    a: astound   **b: rummage**   **c: fathom**

8. My favourite sweater was ruined when moths …………………………...ed our house.

    a: culminate   **b: curator**   **c: infest**

9. At the band's first performance at a festival, they wanted to ……………….....…….. the crowd with their sound.

    a: rummage   **b: astound**   **c: antiseptic**

10. John Smith's role as …………………...…….. allowed him to take care of ancient and priceless artefacts.

    a: relinquish   **b: astound**   **c: curator**

Vocabulary 20

Learn the following words and then answer the questions.

1. **Demean** (v.): humiliate, degrade, disgrace.
   I would not demean myself by cheating in the exam.

2. **Debrief** (v.): to question about a completed mission, undertaking or project.
   NASA debriefed the astronaut about his trip to Mars when he returned to Earth; he reported that he had not found life there.

3. **Emaciated** (adj.): very thin, bony, skeletal.
   After suffering from a serious illness and eating very little, my father was emaciated and it took many months for him to regain weight.

4. **Astute** (adj.): intelligent, shrewd, wise, perceptive.
   Katie made an astute decision to sell her house before the prices went down, and so she made a substantial profit.

5. **Party** (n.): a formal political group; a social gathering; a group of people in a common activity.
   The walking party decided to stop before nightfall to set up camp.

6. **Cagey** (adj.): secretive, evasive, wary, reluctant to give information.
   Camilla was very cagey about where she had been after school, because Mum did not like her hanging about in the park.

7. **Indecision** (n.): the inability to make decisions quickly, hesitation, uncertainty,
   Jane's indecision in front of the goal allowed the defender to tackle her and win the ball.

8. **Putrefy** (v.): decay, rot, decompose, go bad.
   The fruit which was left to rot in the compost began to putrefy and attract flies.

9. **Narrative** (n.): spoken account, story, tale, description.
   The audience was captivated by the soldier's gripping narrative of his escape from an enemy camp.

10. **Obliterate** (v.): destroy, demolish, eliminate.
    The aim of many video games is to obliterate the enemy.

Vocab 20
Cut-and-keep

- demean
- debrief
- emaciated
- astute
- party
- cagey
- indecision
- putrefy
- narrative
- obliterate

Synonym Exercise A

Write the word from the vocab list which is most **similar** in meaning next to each word listed below.

1. Question ....
2. Perceptive ....
3. Tale ....
4. Thin ....
5. Degrade ....
6. Decompose ....
7. Evasive ....
8. Uncertainty ....
9. Destroy ....
10. Group ....

Exercise B

Write the most suitable word from the vocab list in the spaces below. You might need to change the form of the word; for instance, walk might become walked.

1. It is important to store food correctly; meat and fish can .... if not refrigerated.

2. The bully tried to .... the poor girl by making fun of her clothes; she was not intimidated and eventually he stopped.

3. The old sailor was .... about his past life and reluctant to divulge any information, even to his closest friends.

4. The CIA have to .... their agents following undercover and classified operations.

5. The opposition .... announced its election plan, promising lower taxes and greater public spending.

6. After a moment's ...., Kylie replied that she would be honoured to take up the position of CEO.

7. The critics argued that the book's .... was inconsistent and failed to make much sense.

8. The Allied troops were shocked when they reached Nazi Germany and found hundreds of thousands of weak and .... prisoners.

9. The Ancient Egyptians wanted to .... the memory of the pharaoh Hatshepsut by erasing her name and image from all ancient monuments.

10. The remarkably .... lawyer found several minute but significant contradictions in the witness's testimony.

Vocab 20

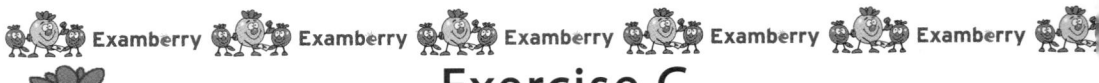

Exercise C

Select the most suitable word from the choice provided.

1. If the hurricane hits the town directly, it will ………………………… all the houses completely.

   a: obliterate   b: indecision   c: emaciated

2. Many lawyers are …………………………… about divulging information to the opposition in case it impacts their case.

   a: bloodshed   b: debrief   c: cagey

3. Elaine was a brilliant and …………………………………. detective; she could solve the most complex crimes.

   a: emaciated   b: astute   c: putrefy

4. The team was ……………………………….ed after the match so that the players could learn from their mistakes.

   a: debrief   b: cagey   c: demean

5. The …………………………………. was a great success, with fun had by all.

   a: emaciated   b: narrative   c: party

6. My dad warned us that if we left the sausage rolls on the picnic table in full sun, they would begin to ……………………………. and be inedible.

   a: putrefy   b: debrief   c: cagey

7. The dog was …………………………. after a long period of neglect.

   a: demean   b: emaciated   c: putrefy

8. Ancient wisdom states that even a wrong decision is preferable to …………………………. .

   a: bloodshed   b: obliterate   c: indecision

9. After the accident, the drivers gave two different ……………………………s of how it had happened.

   a: narrative   b: emaciated   c: debrief

10. If I was a teacher I would not ………………………….. my students by humiliating them in front of the class.

    a: indecision   b: demean   c: cagey

Answers

Vocabulary 1	Vocabulary 2	Vocabulary 3
Exercise A	**Exercise A**	**Exercise A**
1. portray	1. aptitude	1. supremacy
2. curdle	2. heist	2. stability
3. affix	3. manifest	3. provoke
4. nuptial	4. conscientious	4. decisive
5. secluded	5. choreograph	5. wildfire
6. spurious	6. taciturn	6. inventive
7. feline	7. vain	7. phenomenon
8. depression	8. rupture	8. derive
9. disgruntled	9. potter	9. perturb
10. infuriate	10. diligence	10. sanctuary
Exercise B	**Exercise B**	**Exercise B**
1. curdle	1. heist	1. phenomenon
2. secluded	2. vain	2. perturb
3. nuptial	3. choreograph	3. provoke
4. portray	4. conscientious	4. wildfire
5. feline	5. potter	5. stability
6. depression	6. taciturn	6. sanctuary
7. affix	7. aptitude	7. supremacy
8. infuriate	8. rupture	8. inventive
9. spurious	9. diligence	9. decisive
10. disgruntled	10. manifest	10. derive
Exercise C	**Exercise C**	**Exercise C**
1. portray	1. vain	1. perturb
2. nuptial	2. rupture	2. stability
3. feline	3. taciturn	3. inventive
4. depression	4. diligence	4. provoke
5. infuriate	5. conscientious	5. derive
6. affix	6. aptitude	6. wildfire
7. secluded	7. potter	7. decisive
8. curdle	8. manifest	8. phenomenon
9. spurious	9. choreograph	9. sanctuaries
10. disgruntled	10. heist	10. supremacy

© Examberry 2021

Answers

Vocabulary 4	Vocabulary 5	Vocabulary 6	Vocabulary 7
Exercise A	**Exercise A**	**Exercise A**	**Exercise A**
1. henceforth	1. roam	1. unbelievable	1. scruple
2. detest	2. abysmal	2. continuation	2. congregate
3. cautious	3. punctual	3. wither	3. hygienic
4. hallmark	4. enact	4. avenge	4. garnish
5. imply	5. exemplify	5. donor	5. discontinued
6. common sense	6. venture	6. antidote	6. institution
7. broadcast	7. encounter	7. convex	7. anatomy
8. deduct	8. ornamental	8. epiphany	8. equality
9. dweller	9. concave	9. opulent	9. mourn
10. retail	10. catapult	10. literary	10. lapel
Exercise B	**Exercise B**	**Exercise B**	**Exercise B**
1. deduct	1. catapult	1. continuation	1. equality
2. cautious	2. exemplify	2. wither	2. hygienic
3. hallmark	3. enact	3. literary	3. garnish
4. common sense	4. punctual	4. unbelievable	4. anatomy
5. broadcast	5. venture	5. opulent	5. lapel
6. dweller	6. ornamental	6. avenge	6. scruple
7. imply	7. encounter	7. antidote	7. discontinued
8. henceforth	8. abysmal	8. donor	8. congregated
9. detest	9. concave	9. convex	9. mourn
10. retail	10. roam	10. epiphany	10. institution
Exercise C	**Exercise C**	**Exercise C**	**Exercise C**
1. hallmark	1. punctual	1. donor	1. mourn
2. dweller	2. concave	2. unbelievable	2. garnished
3. deduct	3. enact	3. literary	3. scruple
4. detest	4. exemplify	4. wither	4. lapel
5. imply	5. venture	5. avenge	5. hygienic
6. common sense	6. ornamental	6. convex	6. congregated
7. henceforth	7. catapult	7. continuation	7. equality
8. cautious	8. encounter	8. opulent	8. discontinued
9. broadcast	9. abysmal	9. epiphany	9. anatomy
10. retail	10. roam	10. antidote	10. institution

© Examberry 2021

Answers

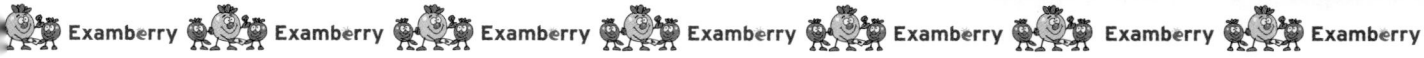

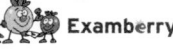

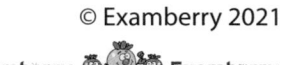

Vocabulary 8	Vocabulary 9	Vocabulary 10	Vocabulary 11
Exercise A	Exercise A	Exercise A	Exercise A

Vocabulary 8 – Exercise A
1. forte
2. lukewarm
3. dominance
4. divinity
5. morgue
6. befriend
7. demeanour
8. slander
9. averse
10. analyst

Vocabulary 9 – Exercise A
1. seldom
2. expose
3. complement
4. prosperous
5. dowry
6. profuse
7. mayhem
8. abide
9. fellowship
10. anticipation

Vocabulary 10 – Exercise A
1. establish
2. advent
3. rational
4. imaginative
5. vault
6. rescind
7. estrange
8. degrade
9. vivacious
10. predator

Vocabulary 11 – Exercise A
1. aggravate
2. generation
3. decrepit
4. briskly
5. odour
6. refine
7. bewildered
8. eloquent
9. charcoal
10. confess

Vocabulary 8 – Exercise B
1. demeanour
2. averse
3. slander
4. befriend
5. dominance
6. morgue
7. forte
8. analyst
9. lukewarm
10. divinity

Vocabulary 9 – Exercise B
1. prosperous
2. profuse
3. complement
4. mayhem
5. seldom
6. dowry
7. anticipation
8. abide
9. fellowship
10. expose

Vocabulary 10 – Exercise B
1. establish
2. imaginative
3. vivacious
4. rational
5. estrange
6. predator
7. vault
8. degrade
9. rescind
10. advent

Vocabulary 11 – Exercise B
1. briskly
2. confess
3. charcoal
4. aggravate
5. bewildered
6. odour
7. eloquent
8. decrepit
9. generation
10. refine

Vocabulary 8 – Exercise C
1. demeanour
2. forte
3. slander
4. lukewarm
5. morgue
6. averse
7. analyst
8. befriended
9. dominance
10. divinity

Vocabulary 9 – Exercise C
1. profuse
2. complement
3. expose
4. mayhem
5. anticipation
6. abide
7. fellowship
8. seldom
9. prosperous
10. dowry

Vocabulary 10 – Exercise C
1. rational
2. advent
3. imaginative
4. predator
5. degrade
6. estrange
7. vivacious
8. establish
9. rescind
10. vault

Vocabulary 11 – Exercise C
1. odour
2. refine
3. generation
4. briskly
5. charcoal
6. confess
7. eloquent
8. decrepit
9. bewildered
10. aggravate

© Examberry 2021

Answers

Vocabulary 12	Vocabulary 13	Vocabulary 14
Exercise A	Exercise A	Exercise A

Vocabulary 12 — Exercise A
1. belittle
2. seclusion
3. eliminate
4. autopsy
5. bacteria
6. integrity
7. accession
8. eminent
9. earshot
10. vulture

Vocabulary 13 — Exercise A
1. accentuate
2. pertinent
3. anarchy
4. ravine
5. pictorial
6. resourceful
7. eavesdrop
8. affiliate
9. carnage
10. gastric

Vocabulary 14 — Exercise A
1. onus
2. bombard
3. orator
4. exuberant
5. truncate
6. loot
7. affectionate
8. thwart
9. conserve
10. amnesia

Vocabulary 12 — Exercise B
1. belittle
2. eminent
3. earshot
4. integrity
5. autopsy
6. bacteria
7. eliminate
8. vulture
9. accession
10. seclusion

Vocabulary 13 — Exercise B
1. ravine
2. resourceful
3. affiliate
4. accentuate
5. eavesdrop
6. pertinent
7. pictorial
8. gastric
9. carnage
10. anarchy

Vocabulary 14 — Exercise B
1. affectionate
2. orator
3. thwarted
4. loot
5. truncate
6. exuberant
7. onus
8. amnesia
9. bombard
10. conserve

Vocabulary 12 — Exercise C
1. bacteria
2. vulture
3. eminent
4. autopsy
5. seclusion
6. belittle
7. integrity
8. earshot
9. eliminate
10. accession

Vocabulary 13 — Exercise C
1. carnage
2. pertinent
3. gastric
4. anarchy
5. affiliate
6. resourceful
7. eavesdrop
8. accentuate
9. ravine
10. pictorial

Vocabulary 14 — Exercise C
1. bombard
2. conserve
3. loot
4. thwart
5. affectionate
6. orator
7. onus
8. amnesia
9. truncate
10. exuberant

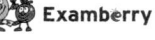

© Examberry 2021

Answers

Vocabulary 15

Exercise A

1. detriment
2. propensity
3. ruthless
4. maul
5. coalition
6. haggard
7. epitome
8. endowment
9. dissect
10. ligament

Exercise B

1. propensity
2. maul
3. ruthless
4. epitome
5. endowment
6. ligaments
7. detriment
8. dissect
9. haggard
10. coalition

Exercise C

1. dissect
2. haggard
3. epitome
4. coalition
5. propensity
6. ligament
7. maul
8. ruthless
9. endowment
10. detriment

Vocabulary 16

Exercise A

1. dissertation
2. delinquent
3. denote
4. equity
5. extension
6. defensible
7. adamant
8. combustion
9. monetary
10. parachute

Exercise B

1. combustion
2. dissertation
3. adamant
4. extension
5. delinquent
6. monetary
7. defensible
8. parachute
9. equity
10. denote

Exercise C

1. parachute
2. monetary
3. combustion
4. dissertation
5. equity
6. denote
7. extension
8. adamant
9. delinquent
10. defensible

Vocabulary 17

Exercise A

1. dire
2. abrasive
3. prudent
4. perpetual
5. storey
6. outcry
7. casket
8. admirable
9. barometer
10. archaeology

Exercise B

1. storey
2. outcry
3. archaeology
4. casket
5. prudent
6. admirable
7. barometer
8. dire
9. perpetual
10. abrasive

Exercise C

1. storey
2. barometer
3. dire
4. archaeology
5. perpetual
6. casket
7. abrasive
8. admirable
9. outcry
10. prudent

© Examberry 2021

Answers

Vocabulary 18

Exercise A

1. throttle
2. outermost
3. blasé
4. intestine
5. platonic
6. grandeur
7. equitable
8. ethical
9. aggrieved
10. denounce

Exercise B

1. throttle
2. denounce
3. aggrieve
4. outermost
5. blasé
6. equitable
7. ethical
8. grandeur
9. platonic
10. intestine

Exercise C

1. platonic
2. denounced
3. blasé
4. ethical
5. grandeur
6. aggrieved
7. intestine
8. throttle
9. outermost
10. equitable

Vocabulary 19

Exercise A

1. strenuous
2. curator
3. culminate
4. relinquish
5. infest
6. fathom
7. frankness
8. astound
9. rummage
10. antiseptic

Exercise B

1. antiseptic
2. frankness
3. infest
4. strenuous
5. astound
6. fathom
7. relinquish
8. rummage
9. culminate
10. curator

Exercise C

1. frankness
2. relinquish
3. culminate
4. antiseptic
5. rummage
6. strenuous
7. fathom
8. infest
9. astound
10. curator

Vocabulary 20

Exercise A

1. debrief
2. astute
3. narrative
4. emaciated
5. demean
6. putrefy
7. cagey
8. indecision
9. obliterate
10. party

Exercise B

1. putrefy
2. demean
3. cagey
4. debrief
5. party
6. indecision
7. narrative
8. emaciated
9. obliterate
10. astute

Exercise C

1. obliterate
2. cagey
3. astute
4. debrief
5. party
6. putrefy
7. emaciated
8. indecision
9. narrative
10. demean

© Examberry 2021